Music in My Heart

and
Borscht in My Blood

An Autobiography
by

Henry Tobias

HIPPOCRENE BOOKS
New York

Excerpts from the following are reprinted with permission by the writers and copyright owners: *The Borscht Belt* by Henry Tobias and Joey Adams; from the *Los Angeles Times* by Art Buchwald (column about Grossinger's); from the *Los Angeles Times* by Charles Champlin ("Surreal Exit to a Unique Career"); from the "Bintel Brief" by Rabbi Jerry Cutler (eulogy on Dick Shawn).

For information, address: Hippocrene Books, Inc.
171 Madison Avenue, New York, NY 10016.

Library of Congress Cataloging-in-Publication Data

Tobias, Henry.
  Music in my heart and borscht in my blood.

  1. Tobias, Henry.   2. Composers—United States—
Biography.   I. Title.
ML410.T517A3   1987   784.5′0092′4 [B]   87-19743
ISBN 0-87052-457-7

Printed in the United States of America.

CONTENTS

ACKNOWLEDGMENTS

Sincere thanks to the following people, without whom this book would not be possible: my wife Sophie Josephine, my daughter Phylis Brown, my grandsons Tim, Mitchell, and Kelly Brown, and my brothers Harry and Milton; and my former bosses, Joey Adams, Leonard Korobkin, Syd Cassyd, Ralph Hancock, Roy Wallenstein; and Bertha Klausner, my literary agent, who encouraged and inspired me for many years to write this book. And, the many well-known friends in show business and the music industry who cooperated with me in interviews, stories, permission to reproduce material and pictures, including: Milton Berle, Eddie Cantor, Georgie Jessell, Red Buttons, Danny Kaye, Alan King, Jerry Lewis, Buddy Hackett, Joey Bishop, Jan Murray, Dick Shawn, Robert Merrill, Henny Youngman, Jackie Gleason, Frank Sinatra, Harry Belafonte, Nat King Cole, Lena Horne, Joe E. Lewis, Tony Bennett, Elvis Presley, Joel Grey, Sid Caesar, Bobby Breen, Jimmy Durante, Sophie Tucker, Rudy Vallee, Mae West, Jackie Mason. Apologies to all those others I forgot to mention.

Thank you,
Henry Tobias

FOREWORD

When Henry Tobias asked me to write a foreword to this book, I gladly accepted, for I've known him almost all my life. HE WAS THERE when I was there.

When I first started playing club dates as a kid at the Hunts Point Palace in the Bronx, HE WAS THERE.

When I played Vaudeville, HE WAS THERE plugging his songs for his publishers. When I appeared in the Earl Carrol Vanities in 1932, HE WAS THERE, writing songs for the show and me. When I was interested in a show called "Off to Buffalo" starring Joe Cook, he called me from Philadelphia and told me he was in the show and that it was folding. They needed money to bring it to New York and asked me to invest. I did. The show closed in one week. My money was no longer there, but Henry was there. (We wrote three songs for the show.) When I needed a theme song for my radio show, "The Gillette Community Sing," HE WAS THERE. When I went to visit my mother at Grossingers, HE WAS THERE—social directing and "toomling"—HE WAS THERE. When I was booked by the William Morris Agency to star at Totem Lodge, HE WAS THERE. When I appeared at the Fountainbleau Hotel in Florida, HE WAS THERE. But after he inadvertently knocked down the microphone after introducing me, HE WAS NO LONGER THERE.

When I opened in Nicky Blair's Carnival Night Club in New York and needed some special material, HE WAS THERE. He and his brothers Charlie and Harry were always there at every opening of mine or wherever they could land a plug for one of their songs. They were known as the best demonstrators of songs. THEY WERE

ALWAYS THERE. And when Henry moved to California in 1972, I WAS THERE. And as president of the Friars Club, I made sure he would be there by making him and his brother Harry lifelong honorary members.

If you love nostalgia, Tin Pan Alley, the Borscht Belt, and how some of my best friends started their show business careers, I strongly suggest you read, laugh and enjoy this book.

Milton Berle

PREFACE

The dictionaries say that a "Preface" may be an introduction to a book, among other uses. Perhaps, because if a book needs to be introduced, that's the only logical place to put it. Too often, though, one reads "apology" in the preface instead of "introduction" and this, it seems to me, should be left out. An apology for inflicting another book on a public already beleaguered by a barrage of books coming off the presses daily is an exercise in futility, ambiguity, and hypocrisy if it is followed by a dull book. If the book is entertaining or the author has something to say that needs saying, then why apologize?

Having never been one who was ready with an apology for the things he inflicted on his audiences, nor falsely modest about his shortcomings, I would be out of character in any role other than pitchman. Since I am primarily a writer of songs and not a writer of books, and also known as an entertainer, among other things, the first question I should answer is, "Why write a book?"

The answer to that is my introduction, my preface.

Well-meaning friends were saying for years, "Henry, why don't you write a book?" Because they knew something of my life and experiences, they never questioned my ability to write a book. They only knew that I had led an exciting and varied career in the music business, resorts, show business, and all phases of entertainment. I had worked with and met such wonderful personalities as Eddie Cantor, Milton Berle, Jimmy Durante, Sophie Tucker, Jerry Lewis, Henny Youngman, Jackie Gleason, Alan King, Joey Bishop, Georgie Jessel, Frank Sinatra, Harry Belafonte, Joe E. Lewis, Mae West,

Rudy Vallee, and many others mentioned in this book. I had led such a varied and exciting career in the music business, Broadway, the Borscht Belt, television, radio, vaudeville, and musical comedy, they all were sure that I could write a very exciting and interesting book.

But I found out the hard way that writing a book was not the same as writing songs. I could write a song in an hour, place it with a publisher, and forget about it. Sometimes if I was lucky the song, through the efforts of the publisher, artist, and luck, would become popular and make some money, but not so with writing a book.

In order to write a book, especially this kind of book, one must spend months, yes, years as I did, researching the material, collecting anecdotes, interviewing hundreds of people and, most important, trying to land a publisher. I have had many of my songs rejected by many publishers and because of my faith in my work and my persistent "never give up" attitude, I sometimes succeeded in getting songs published.

I found the same thing happening when I wrote my first book, *The Borscht Belt*. With the encouragement of my friend and prominent literary agent in New York, Bertha Klausner, I finally wrote a book about my experiences in one-half of my career in the resort industry called "The Borscht Belt." After being turned down by almost every publisher with my first efforts with Ralph Hancock, I finally convinced an old friend, Joey Adams, to collaborate with me and it was he who succeeded in getting it published by Bobbs Merrill in 1969.

Because Joey was not at the same places at the same times as I was, he had to write the book in first person, leaving out much of my best material and making it look as if he wrote it and I was also there.

However, because so much of the material I gave Joey Adams was not used in my first book, and because everyone thought it was HIS story, not MINE, Bertha Klausner convinced me to write this book, my own story of my own life in all phases of show business. I hope you enjoy reading it.

Down Memory Lane

*A*s I sat at my typewriter looking out the window of my office on the eleventh floor of 1650 Broadway in New York City, I couldn't help looking down at Broadway and notice Broadway looking up at me. Suddenly, as I reminisced, I couldn't help realizing that there, in one glance as far as my eyes could see, down to 40th Street and Broadway, went my entire career and life, all revolving around the Great White Way. Starting with the 40th Street WOR Building where I got my first club date from Nat Abramson and received my Social Security number way back in 1937. I tried to remember the places and dates that meant so much to me at the beginning of my career and which all happened right there on the Boulevard of Dreams: Broadway, Times Square, and Tin Pan Alley.

First I saw the New Amsterdam Theatre on 42nd Street, off Broadway. It was in a little Chinese restaurant called the Follies Inn, during the year 1926, that I first started with a small orchestra. I was booked by Ted Rosenthal, a booking agent located at 145 W. 45th Street. It was there I met my future and present wife, Sophie Streiker, who was secretary to Rosenthal. I was only twenty years old and she had just turned fifteen. She helped me get this first job for which I was ever grateful.

My eyes wandered to the corner of 50th Street and Broadway

where Leo Feist Inc., music publishers, were then located. It was there I first played my melody "Katinka" for Phil Kornheiser. He liked it, had Benee Russell write a lyric, and hired me as piano player on staff and writer at $50 per week, half against royalties and half for rehearsing acts and plugging their songs. It was there I first learned how to plug songs. My job was to visit the various vaudeville houses and try to get the acts to feature Feist songs. Their slogan was "You can't go wrong with a Feist song." My first song, "Katinka," was a fairly good-sized hit and so I felt I had established myself as a writer on Tin Pan Alley. I had to prove myself away from my brothers, as both Harry and Charlie were already established writers and two in the family were enough. It wasn't until "Katinka" became well known that brothers Harry and Charlie would seriously listen to my tunes. Out of these hearings came "Miss You," my biggest hit.

It was during my vaudeville theatre visits that I met some of the greats of early vaudeville—Van and Schenck, Sophie Tucker, Belle Baker, Smith and Dale, Milton Berle, Lou Holtz, and others.

As I looked across the street I saw the Brill Building, at 1619 Broadway. It was there I took my first job as pianist and songwriter with Mills Music Co. and had the pleasure of writing with such greats as Billy Rose, Ballard McDonald, Al Dubin, Joe Young, Sam Lewis, Mitchell Parish, Haven Gillespie, and others. It was also there I met Mae West who requested I join her vaudeville act as accompanist, which I did for a short period of time. Jack and Irving Mills willingly lent my services to Mae West in return for her singing a few of their songs in her act—songs like "A Girl That Men Forget," among others.

Down a few blocks, at 48th Street and Broadway, I saw the famous Latin Quarter, formerly the Palais D'Or. So many exciting things happened to me while working at the Latin Quarter and Palais D'Or that I have written them in a special chapter later in this book called "The Latin Quarter."

Way down on the right, off Broadway and 44th Street, I could see the Shubert Theatre advertising "Promises." I recall that it was Billy Rose who gave me my first big break as a songwriter when he asked me to write some songs for his show "Padlocks of 1927," starring the legendary Texas Guinan. It ran for six months at the Shubert Theatre and made me one of the youngest Broadway show songwriters in the business. My experiences with Billy Rose are related in detail later on in this book under the heading BILLY ROSE.

I look out the window and see the building that housed DeSylva, Brown and Henderson on the corner of 49th Street and 7th Avenue, and the old Irving Berlin Publishing Company offices located upstairs in that building above the Chinese restaurant. And there is the old Loew's State Theatre and the famous RKO Palace, where I spent many Monday afternoon matinees writing down new gags by the comedians and later exchanging them with other Social Directors at the "Corn Exchange" drug store on 45th Street, across from the Lowe's State stage door.

Memories, memories, and more memories. But let's start at the beginning. . . .

Chapter 1

How It All Started

I was born in Worcester, Massachusetts, on April 23, 1905, and given the first name of Hyman, later changed to Henry for professional reasons. My father, Max, was a struggling tailor who had decided to leave New York several years before I was born and try his luck out of town. He chose Worcester because a fellow cloak-and-suiter had moved there and painted a pleasant picture of small-town life and steady work as compared to the life in New York City slums. I was the fourth boy in a family of five brothers. My three older brothers, Harry, Charlie, and Nathan, were born in New York City. Milton was born ten years after I was, in Worcester.

Up until I was about ten years old, nothing unusual happened that I can remember other than that I led a very normal kid's life—going to Providence Street School, living on the top of the hill near the Worcester Academy, enjoying the usual children's pleasures: in the winter romping in the high snow, racing downhill with our double-runner sleds; in the summer going to White City at Lake

1

Quinsigamond with the family. I recall my father teaching me to swim the breaststroke for the first time, getting my first taste of hero worship when I was introduced to Jess Willard, the heavyweight champ of the world, at the lake.

My life has been so closely associated with show business that my memories really start with the first day I faced an audience. I was only nine years old and, like other kids attending Hebrew School, I had to recite a poem in my synagogue at the foot of Providence Street Hill. I chose the 23rd Psalm, "The Lord Is My Shepherd." That was my first appearance before an audience. I was petrified. The next big event of my life was when I met Eddie Cantor, but more about that in a later chapter.

We moved back to New York City because my brothers Charlie and Harry chose songwriting as their careers and knew that they could accomplish their ambitions only in the big town. The folks bought a piano and Harry and Charlie encouraged me to learn to play. They said it would be nice if someone in the family could play music as they were both lyric writers.

We moved to the Bronx, first on Simpson Street near Westchester Avenue, then to Minford Place, where I was bar mitzvahed, then near Crotona Park. It was nice living along the park. We had a little taste of the country in the city.

I guess music and showbiz were in my blood for keeps, for next I recall entertaining in P.S. 50 in the Bronx and also at Morris High School, where I was elected 5th and 7th term representative and head of the cheerleading squad. I was the first to appoint a female cheerleader in America. Her name was Sadie Schoenholtz.

My brothers Charlie and Harry were busy writing songs and invited several established songwriters, such as Ray Henderson, Al Sherman, Harry Woods, and others, to our house to write with them. I was fascinated by their work and made up my mind that someday I too would compose songs. However, I hated to practice the elementary lessons in piano playing and after a few years of monotonous scales decided to learn popular songs myself, which I did. I was to regret this move later on, but like so many other kids I was too ambitious and anxious to learn fast, and learning classical music was too slow for me. I got hold of the piano copies of hits of the day like Irving Berlin's "Home" and "You'd Be Surprised," and learned how to play them. I also learned some comedy songs that Eddie Cantor featured. When I knew them well, I felt I was ready to launch my career. I organized my first orchestra with two other

2

fellows from the neighborhood: Murray Brodatz (violin) and Mike Amster (drums). I was at the piano.

We took our first job for the summer. It was at the Shady Grove Hotel in Haines Falls, high up in the Catskills above the Hudson, ten miles from the town of Catskill. We worked for just room and board and a few dollars expense money each week. I soon found out that I was the "life of the party" at the hotel. I had learned a few gags, Eddie Cantor's mannerisms and some of his material, and was always laughing it up, a lanky, skinny, nervous pimple-faced kid. I didn't know then that I was one of the first so-called social directors ("Toomlers"), for that's how most of them started. Toomler, derived from tumult-maker, is Yiddish for a fool or noisemaker who does anything and everything to entertain the customers so that they won't squawk about their rooms or food. In addition to my piano playing, I took it upon myself to arrange the programs for daytime and nighttime activities.

After the summer we started taking engagements around the neighborhood: weddings, bar mitzvahs, Jewish Center dances, and so forth. I kept learning more pop songs, increasing my library, and found I could fake with the rest. My father was still working at the machine, seasonally, and so we all helped in contributing to the family fund. My little jobs were interspersed with selling papers on Sunday at the Bronx Park Subway Station to make a few extra bucks.

In the meantime, brother Harry had written his first successful popular song with William Dillon, the man who wrote "I Wanna Girl Just Like the Girl." The excitement of his first successful song not only brought him financial reward but convinced him that this was his life, and he convinced brother Charlie to join him in the music business. Charlie had many talents and was also smitten by the "Eddie Cantor bug," for he decided not only to make songwriting his profession, but to become a vaudevillian and earn enough money so that he could continue his songwriting activities.

I guess this enthusiasm ran in the family for I kept writing songs and putting them away. The more my brothers discouraged me, the more I was determined to write. You see they felt, as did the folks, that two songwriters in the family were enough.

When I was graduated from Morris High School I decided to stay as close to Tin Pan Alley as I could. I took a job as a shipping clerk with Joe Davis Music Company so that I could be close to and in the music business. I finally realized that I must go out and prove myself before the brothers would give me recognition. I decided to try it on my own.

One day I summoned up enough courage to play some of my melodies for a big publisher, Phil Kornheiser of Feist. In those days a melody writer could play his tunes for a publisher or lyricist and many song hits were written that way. The tunes were written first. Perhaps that is why you recall those beautiful melodies like "Whispering," "Linger a While," "Tea for Two," "Smoke Gets in Your Eyes," and others in that era. To my surprise, Mr. Kornheiser liked a minor melody I played for him. I had written it while working in a nightclub in Harlem. I wrote it in a few minutes and it was a natural melody. He called in Benee Russell, a lyricist, and asked him to write a lyric. Being a minor Russian melody, he came up with the title "Katinka." Feist published it, George Olsen recorded it, and it became a moderate success—selling about one hundred thousand copies, which was considered pretty good in those days—and earned over a thousand dollars for me. I was on my way.

My folks, and particularly Charlie and Harry, were thrilled with my first success. They listened more carefully to the tunes I played for them and finally selected one melody for which they wrote lyrics. It was called "Miss You," and it became a big success when Rudy Vallee recorded it. It looked like the beginning of a new trio, the Tobias Brothers, but unfortunately our careers went in different directions and we were able to collaborate only occasionally and not to "keep it in the family."

On the strength of "Katinka" I was able to secure a job as plugger, pianist, and writer for Feist at a salary of $50 per week plus $50 drawing against my future royalties. I was just out of my teens and thought songwriting was a cinch, but I was so wrong. I found out that song hits come few and far between, and for every popular song you might write, you must write a hundred flops. I kept playing the piano at night whenever I could get a club job with my band.

From Feist I went to work at Mills Music Co. with the same financial arrangements. They accepted a song I wrote with Billy Rose and Al Dubin called "Pretty Little Thing." The song never became a hit but it introduced me to that fabulous character Billy Rose. It was during my early plugging days for Feist and Mills that I got to meet many of the greats of show business and Tin Pan Alley. My job was to rehearse the acts and contact them at the different vaudeville houses around New York, so I had occasion to meet

Milton Berle, Harry Richmond, Smith and Dale, Van and Schenck, and all the greats of that time.

I have learned in my many years of songwriting that although one can always improve a melody, sometimes it will hurt the tune if you change it and lose some of the natural spontaneous melodic qualities. I wrote some of my best tunes easily. "Katinka" came to me in a few moments of fooling around at the piano on a minor chord in a nightclub in Harlem where I was working. It was later than 3:00 A.M. and I could hardly keep my eyes open, but I made sure I wrote down the opening strain, otherwise I might forget it. My best tune, "Miss You," came to me quickly and naturally, and I have found out that some of my best melodies were those that came easily. Irving Berlin never could play the piano and knew nothing of harmony, construction, theory, etc., but he did all right.

BILLY ROSE

My first meeting with Billy Rose was in early 1927 when he was reaching the top of the list of pop songwriters. He had to his credit such big hits as "Barney Google," "That Old Gang Of Mine," and many others, and was known in Tin Pan Alley as the best businessman of all writers (publishers feared him), as an egomaniac (many short men have a Napoleonic complex to overcome their feelings about short height), and as a really tough guy. I was fresh with enthusiasm as a result of my first popular song hit, "Katinka," and one day I got together enough courage to approach him at Remick's Music Publishing Co.

I timidly said, "Mr. Rose, my name is Henry Tobias. I write melodies. I wondered if you might be interested in hearing some of them."

To my surprise Billy answered, "Sure, kid, I'm always looking for new and fresh tunes. Come up to my apartment tonight and bring along your best melodies and we'll give a listen."

I was so excited when I got home. I looked through my book of original tunes (I always wrote my melodies in a book, then put them away for some future time). I picked out my best tunes, a few dozen, and ran downtown to West 54th, corner of Seventh Avenue, where Billy resided. He introduced me to a revered and well known lyricist by the name of Ballard McDonald, who had written many Broadway shows.

They listened to my melodies. Billy checked off a half dozen and then told me that he and Ballard were writing a Broadway show for Texas Guinan called "Padlocks of 1927," and if I were willing, they would write a half dozen songs with me and use them in the show—no box office royalty, just song royalties. They also said they were writing with two other melody writers, Jesse Greer and Lee David. In those days I would have written the score for nothing, just to get the prestige and chance to write with Billy and Ballard. We wrote six songs that were used in the show. My name was prominently displayed on the copies and on the program, but there were very little royalties. I later found out he used this method in order to avoid paying us box-office royalties. By bringing in new and young song-writers, he would not pay box office, just a small royalty. This was one method of "brain-picking," for usually producers would pay some royalty fee every week for the use of the songs, but we all knew Billy's reputation for being a hard businessman and did not object or beef. I was very grateful for this opportunity to write a show, and more.

Billy invited me to his home for breakfast one day, and there I met his charming wife, Fanny Brice, a great comedienne on her own. They had just married. She was a grand person. No one could understand this marriage. Billy, a little, hard-punching, fast-moving wheeler and dealer, ambitious man, married to this great, tall, kind, and successful star. Those who knew Billy realized that this was but one of his steps up the ladder.

It was during breakfast—Fanny was serving scrambled eggs and bacon—when Billy remarked, "Say, Henry, this might be a good idea for a song, 'While I'm Cooking Breakfast for the One I Love.' Here's a dummy, and get busy with a tune." I always envied Billy's talent as a speed stenographer. He was a world's champ when he was secretary to Bernard Baruch. He would sit and scribble notes. When I looked at them, I couldn't decipher them as they were his rapid shorthand notes.

I worked on a melody but Billy was not satisfied with the release. It was only an eight-bar melody but he was a tough man to please, a perfectionist to the last degree. I always wrote my tunes easily. If they didn't come easily, they were no good to me but he didn't believe in that. He called it lazy writing and kept sending me back to try and try again. After several weeks of trying he finally accepted a middle strain. The song was used in Fanny Brice's picture for Warner Brothers entitled "Be Yourself."

Billy was a hard man, but a tremendous success in everything he undertook. First as a songwriter. When he went as far as he could, he became a successful producer and nightclub owner. From there to buying theatres, and from there to Wall Street where they say he became the second largest stockholder of A.T.& T.

MAE WEST

I first met Mae West when I was a piano player for Mills Music Co. at the beginning of my songwriting career. I had written my first song hit, "Katinka," in 1927, and my first Broadway show about that time. I approached Mills with a song they liked that I wrote with Billy Rose and Al Dubin and asked them for a job as a piano plugger. We made a deal for half salary and half drawing account against my songwriting. They had first choice on all new songs. The big stars always rehearsed at the music publishers; in return they would feature that publisher's songs.

One day Mae West came in and asked for a rehearsal pianist. I was assigned to her. She took a liking to me. Let me explain at this time that I don't know why. I was a skinny, tall, nervous kid with pimples. All I thought of was my work, my songs, and my new wife. I had just been married to my teenage sweetheart. We had kept company for several years and on the strength of my "Katinka" royalties and job with Mills, we could afford to get married, so we did.

Mae West was a notorious sexpot known up and down Broadway at that time. When the song pluggers and writers would talk of their escapades with women, Mae West's name always came up. First she had that reputation and now she had decided to go into vaudeville and use a band for half her act; the other half was to be a dramatic presentation with her as Cleopatra. She asked me to join her act temporarily as she only had a few weeks' bookings, then she planned to go into her first Broadway show, "Sex." My publisher gladly consented. It meant more money for me so I said okay, although my wife, having heard of Mae's reputation with men, did not approve. And so at our first appearance in vaudeville, in Passaic, New Jersey, my wife made sure she would be around to keep an eye on me.

Mae West, in my opinion, was never a great actress. She was always playing herself in anything she did. However, her own self was so peculiar, so sexy, so different, so daring, she became a star. I recall only two incidents with her that might be of interest. Mae West at the start of her vaudeville career was not a woman of means. She had a man with her who was her manager, but everyone knew it was her man, although no one knew if they were married. His name was Mr. Timothy.

He wore a black derby, always smoked a cigar, limped on one leg, and never left her side. He probably knew of her reputation with men and was constantly on the watch that she didn't go astray. Her clothes were not expensive; as a matter of fact they were quite shabby, and her jewelry was phony and gaudy. One day my wife came backstage to visit me and I introduced her to Mae, who admired the red dress my wife wore. She had the nerve to ask my wife if she would let her wear it to Christmas dinner that night with Timothy. My wife, being a good schnook, agreed, and sat around between shows in Mae West's dirty kimono, while Mae went out to dinner with her man.

During our performance at the Proctor's Newark Theatre one day, Mae decided to watch the movie between shows and invited me and the comedy star of the show, Al Herman, to watch the movie with her. We sat in the back of the orchestra in the dark, me on one side of Mae and Al on the other. I noticed Al and Mae were kind of close and lovey dovey, holding hands, rubbing knees together, and playing hanky panky. I also noticed in the dark a hovering figure with a Derby and cigar. I knew who it was, it was Timothy looking for his Mae. In the dark he spotted her, walked into the aisle over my feet, slapped her in the face, grabbed her by the hand and yanked her out of her seat. She never went to a movie with any of us again.

Her tremendous success on Broadway, I claim, was a freak. She was playing herself all the time, but never had the public ever seen such a character and wouldn't believe it was her real self; they thought she was acting. Believe me, I never saw Mae West in any vehicle, show or movie, that she wasn't playing herself.

Chapter 2

The Borscht Belt Alumni

*I*forgot to write about another important phase which had a big influence in my life—the "Borscht Belt."

After getting a taste of the Catskills for two summers, I landed a job at an adult summer camp called Camp Everett in Taconic, Connecticut. I had put together some of my high school friends and we formed a small orchestra—Jerry Drexler at trumpet, Eli Steuer at drums, and Harry Zimmerman at sax. We auditioned and won the job.

Being the life of the party at Camp Everett, I was given additional duties as social director and as such had to hire a local staff. I made my drummer, Eli Steuer, my assistant, for he was popular with the girls, and this was more important than playing the drums.

While auditioning for a dramatic director I met a most unusual character—a tall, skinny, sad-eyed Russian by the name of Mischa Auer. He was a grandson, on his mother's side, of the famous violin teacher Leopold Auer. His father was an officer in the Czar's army

9

and when the Revolution came, his father was killed and he and his mother had to run away to try and seek refuge with her father, Leopold Auer, in America.

Mischa's mother died in Turkey and while still in his teens he had to bury his mother en route and make his way to America, where he lived and was brought up by his grandfather. He studied dramatics, made a few appearances with Bertha Kalich, and was looking for a summer job. I immediately took a liking to him which started a friendship of a lifetime.

With all his dramatic ability, Mischa had a flare for comedy and it was this talent that finally won him fame in Hollywood as a comedy character actor. Later on, after he had established a name in the movies, Mischa and I got together and did a vaudeville act. I wrote it for him and accompanied him on the piano. He was a beautiful human being and I cherished his friendship.

If my memory seems to be skipping from winter to summer resorts and back again, it's because my whole life and career has been skipping from one phase of show business to another—from music and show business to the Borscht Belt.

The only job I did stick to for many summers was at Totem Lodge. As I look back and realize how many years I stayed at that one place (from 1927 to 1938, then from 1942 to 1957), I realize that the borscht must have gone into my blood for many years. It was not only the glamour, excitement, and enjoyment of creating, producing, acting, and being the big boss in the summer resort business, but also it was a certain security that made it possible for me to freelance in the winter and do the many things I wanted to do such as write, play with my orchestra, be in vaudeville, etc. I guess my career was similar to the male lead in the picture "Marjorie Morningstar" starring Gene Kelly, who preferred to be a big man in a small summer hotel than a small man in Hollywood. Eddie Cantor, my brothers, and my best friends have all told me and were convinced that I might have been a big man in Hollywood if I had chosen to give up my resort career but I didn't and so no regrets.

The first few years with big staffs our program consisted of campfires, masquerades, kiddie nights, vice-versa nights, hillbilly nights, square dances, concerts, quizzes, dramatic shows, movies, amateur nights, staff nights, and Saturday Night Big Vaudeville Shows. I was the first to introduce bands on stage in resorts and stage presentations with talent presented in front of the band.

As time went on the resort owners realized that the expense and upkeep of a complete staff for the ten weeks of summer was too great to warrant the results. So slowly but surely my staff grew smaller and to replace them, we brought in outside talent for Saturday night. These were usually friends we or the staff knew. For instance, Benney Lessey and Julie Oshines would invite Phil Silvers, Rags Ragland, and Joey Faye up for the weekend, and they would cause a riot doing the old burlesque bits, as these were the greatest burlesque comedians of all times.

My brother Charlie would come up with other well-known songwriters and present "The Songwriters on Parade." The smaller hotels which could not afford a big staff started booking outside talent. This was the beginning of the Borscht Circuit and became an important part of show business.

Almost every big name in show business received his start in the Borscht Circuit. The list of funny men from the mountains included Jerry Lewis, Sid Caesar, Phil Silvers, Danny Kaye, Phil Foster, Henny Youngman, Buddy Hackett, Red Buttons, Dick Shawn, and many others. Since the end of burlesque and the death of vaudeville, the Borscht Circuit has been the birthplace of new talent. Where else can new talent get the opportunity to learn to do everything in show business, to try out new material, and to get the experience so necessary in show business?

There is still no substitute for experience.

Not only comics and musical talent grew up in the Borscht Belt, but also dramatic and writing talents received an opportunity to prove their talents—John Garfield, Moss Hart, Max Liebman, Dory Schary, Elia Kazan, and many more too numerous to mention at this time.

As the demand for weekend talent in the Borscht Belt grew and grew, I found it more difficult each year to hire a permanent staff or stock company, for why should a young comic or singer take a ten-week job for a few hundred dollars and room and board when one could play one-night engagements at different hotels and get more money? Bookers like Charlie Rapp, who handled many hotels, could guarantee an act five or more dates a week and during the summer play fifty or sixty hotels. Even at a small fee this would mount up and surely be a larger income than could be earned at one spot all summer. Also the guests, particularly the season guests, would get tired of listening to the same voice or seeing the same face week in and week out. This was an opportunity for the hotel owners to give the guests more diversified entertainment at lower prices than it cost them to house and feed a staff for the summer. So little by little the resorts turned to one-nighters and smaller staffs.

The weekly program kept changing with the times. The weekend revues and musical comedies were replaced by the three-act vaudeville show—a dance team, a girl singer and a stand-up comic. From this early beginning came new comedians and faces: Dick Shawn, Buddy Hackett, Joey Bishop, Phil Foster, Jackie Mason, Sam Levinson, and many others. The need for audience participation became less and less as the entertainment increased. The old masquerade and costume nights were replaced by champagne and dance contests (led by the dance team.)

THE BORSCHT BELT

The "Borscht Belt" is a nickname given to the resorts located mostly in the northeastern part of our country, specifically the Catskill Mountains located about one hundred miles north of New York City, and the Adirondacks, the Berkshires, the Poconos, and the White Mountains in New England.

When an author appears on promotional tours he speaks of them as "The Chicken Circuit," because chicken is served at most of the banquets. And when an athlete or any sports celebrity appears in public at dinners he says he just appeared on the "Grapefruit Circuit," because most of his dinners start with grapefruit. Back in the old days, about which this book is mainly written, when a performer worked in the mountain resorts in the Catskills or in other Jewish clientele-dominated resort hotels, he would refer to them as the "Borscht Belt," for borscht was one of the most popular Jewish dishes served at these hotels.

The name stuck and became a common expression among performers. The theatrical bible, *Variety,* used it often and made it official. It was used with respect and love and never in a derogatory manner. That is why Joey Adams and I refused to change the title of our original Borscht Belt book even though leading hotel owners and operators such as Jennie Grossinger, and Ray Parker of the Concord, and others asked us to change the name as they felt they had spent millions to build their hotels from little boarding houses to million-dollar enterprises, and by calling it the Borscht Belt we were tearing them down and making fun of them. This is ridiculous. It is like Lincoln denying that he was born in a log cabin. We did not make fun of nor did we denigrate the resort industry. We were born in it, worked in it, and loved it, for where else in this crazy profession would we have such freedom of expression on the stage in front of such fabulous, receptive audiences?

It all started back in the early part of the century when the Jewish immigrants came from Russia and other European countries to New York City. Some of them were farmers back home and didn't like city living, others were not well and needed fresh country air. So they migrated to the nearest country, hills, mountains, and farms, mostly located about one hundred miles north of New York City in the beautiful Catskill Mountains, where the quaint and rural towns of Liberty, Lock Sheldrake, Ferndale, Kiamesha Lake, White Lake, and others were located.

Most of them started as farmers, with Papa taking care of the cows and chickens and Mama taking in a few boarders to enhance the income. Pretty soon the boarders were bringing in more than the cows and chickens, and so they became boarding houses. They competed with one another desperately for business. However, they could not afford any entertainment, so they drafted and depended upon their staff and help. The waiters, busboys, bellhops, lifeguards, chambermaids—anyone who could entertain—became performers on the side. Whoever had any talent was called upon.

And so began the careers of many of the top stars and comedians today. However, they (and I mean most of them) did not start with the names they use today. They all started with their real names. For instance, if I were to ask you who are the following people today, how many would you recognize?

David Kaminsky! I'll save you time and trouble. He became DANNY KAYE. When I appeared at a Florida condominium recently, I asked the same question, and when an old lady shouted after jumping out of her seat with excitement, "DANNY KAYE!" I asked, "How do you know?" She screamed, "I'm his mother!" How was I to know that Danny's mother lived in Florida? (More of Danny later.)

Who is Aaron Schwatt today?—That's right, you're wrong. He's RED BUTTONS. Did you know that Red started as a bellhop in a small kosher hotel in Greenfield Park? A kosher hotel is where neither milk nor dairy food is served with the meat, for religious purposes. Red was making only a few bucks a week as a bellhop and needed more money, so he figured out a way. He filled his fountain pen full of cream and sold it at 25 cents a squirt for those who wanted cream in their coffee. He was the first cream bootlegger. Here is a tough one. Who is Irving Kniberg today? I'll help you. Irving became ALAN KING. He took the first three letters of his second name and switched it. When I first asked Alan how he ever became a Social Director and Toomler, he told me, "When I left high school my father bought me a rocking chair and sat me in the corner every night and filled my mouth full of marbles. I told one joke—spit out a marble. I kept spitting out the marbles one by one and when I lost all my marbles and fell off my rocker, then I became a Social Director."

Here's another I'll bet you don't know. Who is Moishe Miller today? Moishe Miller started as a singer at Grossinger's. In order to make a few extra bucks he moonlighted. On Saturday night, after his performance, he would sneak out of the stage door and run over to a nearby hotel or "kochalane" and sing. He did this every week until Jennie Grossinger caught him and said: "Moishe, I don't mind you singing at another hotel, but must you eat here?" Later an enterprising agent by the name of Moe Gale wandered into Grossinger's, became his manager, changed his name to ROBERT MERRILL, got him his first break on NBC's "Opera of the Air," and from there it was straight to the Met. Ever since then the Nevele Hotel, the President Hotel, the Laurels Country Club, and at least half a dozen others lay claim to Bob making his debut in their barns. More of him later.

It was a long hard road for Joey Gottlieb, who first worked in the mountains during the summer of 1938, at the "cockamamie" Loch Sheldrake Hotel. The Gottlieb Trio was offered eight dollars a head, plus room and scraps. The morning after Labor Day they went to collect their salary and found the place deserted—office, kitchen, everything. "I was glad I had taken a stand," says Joey. "I had insisted laundry had to be included. They said okay because they knew they weren't going to pay me anyway. In the end it worked out about even." A few flops later, Joey Gottlieb changed his name to JOEY BISHOP. "If it weren't for the few laughs I got," he says, "I might have become a rabbi. But it's just as well I'm not. How would that sound, Rabbi Bishop?" More of Joey later.

Jerome Levitch's birth certificate was written with a stick of greasepaint, and his playpen was the hills of Fallsburgh and Loch Sheldrake. His father, Danny Levitch (alias Lewis), was a Jolson-type singer, and Mama Rae was a piano player. Every summer when his father answered the call of the mountains, the little son of Levitch was included in the deal. At fourteen he was a tearoom boy at Brown's and while the world didn't yet know of Jerome's existence, it's for sure that the owners of Brown's did. Born with a funny bone, he would drop a whole tray of peach melbas or make a three-point landing in a pot of mashed potatoes for laughs. On a cold night he might even start a fire in the tearoom—and it didn't have a fireplace!

He pestered his father all summer for jokes and by Labor Day was set to make his mark on immortality. Mom and Pop tried keeping him out of show business as long as they could, but they couldn't. So the kid adopted his parents' name to become JERRY LEWIS, the record pantomime act, and Danny and Rae gave in and got him booked into a saloon in Jersey for a fin a night.

On opening night they decided to telephone the club to find out how he did. They didn't want to say who was calling lest they make Jerry nervous, but they knew they could tell how things had gone by the way he sounded. So Danny hit on the idea of disguising his voice and pretending to be a booker who wanted to offer Jerry a job. "Hello," he crooned into the receiver. "Is this Jerry Lewis? This is Al Rock, the agent. I liked your act tonight and would like to use you on some of my dates."

"Gee, thanks a lot, mister," Jerry breathed excitedly, "but how can you like my act? I haven't been on yet." More about Jerry later on.

When Francine Lassman divorced Xaviar Cugat, she retained custody of her stage name, ABBE LANE. After all, how would it look for an alumni of the Jewish Alps, who comes from Brooklyn, to be billed as Francine Lassman, the Latin Bombshell?

Abbe's first appearance on stage had far from a Latin beat. It had more of a Borscht belt. Her parents, Gracie and Abby Lassman, were friends of mine and I arranged for them to manage the canteen concession for the summer at Totem Lodge. Naturally their luggage included their daughter. Fourteen-year-old Francine was overdeveloped for her age—in fact, for any age. She was the Jewish Dolly Parton of that day. Mommy was anxious for her to become a star, but the kid showed more cleavage than talent. At any rate, you can't keep a stage mother down, and Gracie was the best.

She nagged away until finally I stuck Francine into one of my amateur shows. She did so well that I immediately set her for my

Saturday Night Extravaganza. Although it took Cugat to make her, a star, that is, I still claim I developed her—talent, that is. Or maybe it was just that the borscht and sour cream went to her chest.

MILTON BERLE

Although Milton Berle denies that he ever worked in the Borscht Belt (he might never have worked as a regular staff member), he certainly appeared many times as a guest star at many of the leading hotels after he became a star, especially Grossinger's, where Ma Berle lived during the summer, and the Concord, and also the Totem Lodge, where I worked for years. His real name is Milton Berlinger and like so many others he changed his name so that it would be easier to remember and easier to read on the theatre marquee. Although I have no anecdotes to relate about his appearances at resorts, I have nevertheless developed a fond affection for Milton through the years as a friend and would like to relate how I came to know him and how we developed our friendship.

I first met Milton when he was appearing as a youngster (about twelve years old) at the Hunts Point Palace in the Bronx, New York. In those days when I lived in the Bronx, being a cousin of Eddie Cantor through marriage, I was always interested in show business and show people, and visited the Hunts Point Palace every time they did a vaudeville show. Later when I wrote my first song hit, "Katinka," I was hired by Leo Feist to become a song plugger and staff writer. One of my duties was to visit the various vaudeville houses and contact the acts to try to get them to feature Leo Feist songs. We became better friends and later I wrote a few songs with Milton, including his theme for his first Gillette radio show, entitled, "Here Comes the Berle." When he was about to open in the Carnival Night Club run by Nicky Blair, he asked me to write some special material for him.

When Milton moved to California, he mellowed considerably and matured a great deal. He used to be brash and a tough guy to work with, but age and success and security did much to soften and mellow him, and today he has become one of the most beloved and certainly one of the most talented and best-known comedians in our business. He has done more benefits than anyone and was just re-elected President of the Beverly Hills Friars Club for the fifteenth time.

His friendship to me and my brothers Harry and Charlie has been one of our most valued possessions. He has shown it many times and in many ways. Most recently, he appeared at my brother Harry's ninetieth birthday party and made the event a most memorable evening.

His latest appearance as star of our Loving Tribute to Eddie Cantor which I produced at the Friars Club for the Eddie Cantor B'nai B'rith Lodge on September 15, 1986, was one of his greatest performances, for he loved Eddie Cantor and told many anecdotes of those good old vaudeville days. We shall always be grateful for his many favors, kindnesses and most importantly, his friendship through the years.

MORE BORSCHT BELT

The Borscht Belt, which cradled some of the biggest names in show business, was a handsome ghetto unto itself that consisted of a string of summer camps, hotels, and bungalows in the Catskill and Adirondack Mountains. The resort owners were really farmers who boarded a few city folk come summer and made good before they knew it. They were experts on cows and chickens but they knew from borscht about show business.

As the roomers increased and manure turned into paydirt, these farmers resented having to hire musicians and entertainers to amuse their guests. To the farmers, entertainers were the "free eaters" (*oomzisterger fressers* in Yiddish translation), who were necessary evils needed to keep up with their competitors on the next farm.

In the early days, when Moss Hart "starred" at Camp Copake, Dore Schary jazzed up Grossinger's and Danny Kaye was more important to White Roe Lake than pumpernickel on a Sunday morning, the social director had to be producer, director, writer, actor, song and dance man, emcee, comedian, scenic designer, electrician, stage manager, stagehand, and sometimes waiter and gigolo. After the show he had to mingle with the guests, dance with the fat old women and romance the "Carlottas" ("Dogs"). In addition, he was the "Shadchon," or marriage broker.

But these were only his evening chores. During daylight he doubled as sports and activities director. If he was a big shot he had a permanent staff to help him out, consisting of one other skinny fella, who also doubled in such jobs as tennis pro, basketball player, lifeguard, and busboy. Most of these stars got paid off in meals and a place to sleep, usually cozily situated in a basement storeroom or if they were at the top of their profession—in a stuffy attic. Alan King's bedroom at the White Roe Hotel was a cot onstage.

Today these lettuce patches are billion-dollar, year-round resorts and they boast million-dollar show budgets on a par with Las Vegas. The Concord Hotel pays more money for a star for one night than the combined weekly salaries that Eddie Cantor, Will Rogers, W. C. Fields, Bert Williams, and Fanny Brice got for doing the Ziegfeld Follies of 1925.

JAN PEERCE started with his real moniker, Pinky Pearlmutter, as a violinist at the Breezy Hill Hotel, where he got five bucks more than the other musicians because he also did vocals. Following summer after summer at the President, the Waldmere and the Kiamesha Lake Inn, Jan finally gave up his career as a future Heifitz. As he tells it, "I was one of three violinists working with Abe Pizik's band at a benefit at the Astor Hotel. It was the fiftieth anniversary party for Weber and Fields and all the top show people were present. Suddenly there was a lull and Abe convinced the emcee to let me sing one song, "La donna e' mobile." A few minutes later a waiter told me that Roxy wanted to see me. He had asked me to come to his office the next day. Right away I changed my name to Jan Peerce, threw away my fiddle, cancelled my plans to work for Joe Slutsky at the Nevele that summer and immediately began working in the Roxy Theatre. Soon after that I was at the Met."

DANNY KAYE

Danny Kaye who died recently claimed the undisputed title "King of the Catskills." His first job was as part of the entertainment staff at White Roe Lake in 1933. The staff was headed by "Fishel" Goldfarb, now a very successful businessman, and a pal of Danny's throughout his life. Twenty-year-old Danny learned his trade the hard way, appearing in one play a week and a different variety show every evening. He entertained at breakfast, lunch, and dinner, and then rehearsed all through the night.

During Danny's fifth season fate stepped in. A dance duo decided they needed a third artist. "With a little training we can teach Danny where to put his feet," the ballerina commented with mild enthusiasm. That's how Danny became a dancer. The group was given the elite title "The Three Terpsichoreans."

With the addition of this new dimension, Danny leaped from White Roe Lake to Camp Tamiment as chief emcee, under the direction of Max Liebman. He worked as singer, dancer, juvenile lead, character actor, villain, comic and all-around Toomler. Although it was hardly a training ground for a future movie star, Danny has the Catskills to thank for everything. He segued from stooging in theatres to playing in Abe Lyman's Orchestra; from traveling to Japan, China, Siam, and points east as a dancer in 1934, to begging two-week bookings in third-rate Greenwich Village nightclubs. But David Daniel Kaminsky's name and luck changed only when he met Max Liebman, a former resort bookkeeper then in charge of entertainment at Camp Tamiment.

It was Max who also took an ambitious saxophone player from the Vacationland Hotel in Swan Lake and refined him into the Bigtime, high-class TV comic, Sid Caesar. It was also Max Liebman who first unleashed Danny Kaye's comedic talents by casting him in the Yiddish version of "The Mikado."

Danny owed not only his public success but also much of his private happiness to the mountains. During the winter, he worked for Dr. Samuel Fine, a dentist in the Brownsville section of Brooklyn to which Danny had migrated from Russia with his parents. He never noticed the boss's bright-eyed daughter Sylvia until he found her slaving over a hot piano writing special material for a production at Camp Tamiment. In 1940 Danny Kaye and Sylvia Fine were married.

It was still another mountaineer who handed Danny his first chance on Broadway. Moss Hart saw his performance at La Martinique Nightclub on 57th Street and wrote in a part for him in Kurt Weill's "Lady in the Dark," starring Gertrude Lawrence. Danny, Moss Hart, and Broadway clicked from their very first meeting.

BUDDY HACKETT

Leonard Hacker began his professional life in the Coney Island striptease act "Tirza and Her Wine Bath" because the boss let him drink the leftover grape. He became Buddy Hackett when "my agent, Abby Greshler, changed my name at the time I auditioned for the part of 'Henry Aldrich' and lost out to Ezra Stone. I don't know why he changed it. It was a perfectly good name and my father was a good upholsterer."

Like everybody else, Buddy doubled in the dining room during those lean summers. "I never was a good waiter," he insists. "If there was a long line in the kitchen I'd go back to my station and say, 'We ain't got it. Pick sumpthin' else.' Or I'd start 'toomling' in the kitchen and the waiters would forget the customers were waiting."

Our hero made the transition to comedian when a regularly scheduled comic failed to show up. "I was sixteen and the five dollars looked good," Hackett grins. "It was a disaster. They not only didn't laugh, but it looked as though they were comin' up onstage to kill me. I finished out the season in another hotel—but as a waiter!"

The following Memorial Day he rammed a car into a hotel porch in Swan Lake just to get attention. On July Fourth he stuffed dry cereal into the dining room fan and roared when the maitre d' turned it on and created an indoor snowstorm. His biggest job was lifeguard at Grossinger's, and he couldn't even swim.

MOSS HART

Out of the summer camps in the twenties and thirties emerged such illustrious figures as Don Hartman, Dore Schary, Lorenz Hart, Garson Kanin, Arthur Kober, and Moss Hart.

Moss Hart had painful memories of his Catskill apprenticeship. "Social directing," he wrote in his book *Act One,* "provided me with a lifelong disdain and a lasting horror of people in the mass seeking pleasure and release in packaged doses. Perhaps the real triumph of these summers was the fact that I survived them at all. Not so much in terms of emergency with whatever creative faculties I possess unimpaired, but in the sense that my physical constitution withstood the strain, for at the end of each camp season I was always fifteen to twenty pounds lighter and my outlook on life just about that much more heavily misanthropic."

He hated the campfire nights because he had to lead the community sing and drag out blankets and wood for the fire as well as franks and marshmallows. But what made him want to sink into the earth was the "boy-and-girl" number he had to do, complete with ukelele and a fat female guest on his knee.

Game nights killed him altogether. "It is not easy to feel the proper compassion for a shy girl or an ugly duckling when you're tied into a sack with her and are hobbling down the social hall to the finish line," Hart recalled. "On the contrary, rolling a peanut along the floor side by side with a bad-complexioned girl with thick glasses and unfortunate front teeth does nothing to kindle the fires of pity within you, but instead makes you want to kick her right in her unfortunate teeth."

Another torment for Hart was the forced nightly gallantry. One rule that could never be broken under any circumstances was that the male members of the social staff had to dance only with the ugly females. There were sound reasons for this. Every summer camp had two or three women to every man, so the shrewd camp owners met the problem head-on by hiring help whose prime qualification was that they were good dancers. If a musician didn't know his sax from a hole in the ground and if the waiter sloshed hot cabbage soup down the neck of a guest who was staying ten weeks, it didn't matter so long as he "mixed and mingled" well in the social hall.

The big trouble lay in the fact that these college kids, our future doctors, lawyers, and dentists, disliked dancing with the "pots" or "beasts," as they called them. This meant that the full responsibility for the love life and social life of the "beasts" was in the hands of the social directors. This was what forever spoiled the pleasure of dancing for Moss Hart. "For six whole years," Moss complained, "I danced with nothing but the pots, and that was enough to make me welcome the glorious choice of sitting down for the rest of my life."

Certain of Hart's friends suspect that those grueling hot weather sessions, forcibly entertaining lonesome, sweaty young things, bred in him a deep distaste for marriage. He finally did get married to Kitty Carlisle, but not until he was forty-five.

SAM LEVINSON

Sam Levinson was one of the few who made it without bobbing his name. He figured that if Gentiles like Danny Thomas and Jimmy Durante didn't change their noses, he could stick with his inheritance.

The recollections of this ex-schoolteacher, who worked his way through college as a musician at summer resorts, are only beautiful: "Even in those days the mountains had everything: girls, bedbugs, handball, chicken (for ten weeks straight one summer), milk hot from the hot cow, swimming in a pool about the same size as in the picture postcard, and nature—manure at my window.

"It seemed to me at the time that I was immortal. Guests came and went but I stayed on forever. I listened each Sunday to the great debate: 'If we leave at seven in the morning, we can beat the afternoon rush.' 'But we are entitled to lunch.' 'But after lunch the rush starts.' 'So we can stay till the evening.' 'But that means we may have to wait till dinner and they'll charge us five dollars for dinner. Besides, at night you meet the rush that stayed on to beat the rush, so let's stay on till Monday.' 'What! And pay them for an extra day? Besides, the longer you stay, the bigger the tip!' "

Funny lines Sam Levinson remembers:

BELLHOP:"You're not going to forget me, Mr. Harris?"

MR. HARRIS:"No, I'll write you regularly."

PROUD MOTHER:"My daughter won a Cha Cha scholarship at the Nevele."

"The place is just what I expected: soft breezes, beautiful evenings, soft music—and no men."

SIGN IN BATHROOM:"Watch your children. Don't throw anything in the bowl."

Says Sam, "I remember my father wrote me twice a week and as part of the address (he copied from an ad). he included, "LG RMS, ALL IPMTS, ALL SPTS, 75 M.N.Y., RSNBLE."

Sam adds, "I don't think I did much for the mountains but they did plenty for me. They took me out of the tenements for several summers, provided me with tuition for college, and much good subject material for my career in comedy. Let's give the little hills a big hand."

BOB HOPE

Whenever I served as Master of Ceremonies in my long career and had to introduce someone of importance, I would invariably begin by saying: "This man or woman needs no introduction". . . . Now I mean it when I say: BOB HOPE needs no introduction and it would be ludicrous for me to try to write anything about this man that hasn't been written before.

However as he made his first and only appearance in the Borscht Belt a few summers ago at Brown's Hotel in Lock Sheldrake, I would be remiss if I did not include the story behind his booking at this hotel. This story has never been told before and therefore deserves to be printed.

First let me explain that BROWN'S HOTEL was owned and run by Charlie and Lillian Brown. Charlie passed away a few years ago and his wife Lillian still runs the hotel. Her one ambition in life was to outshine Jennie Grossinger who at that time was justifiably called "The Queen of the Catskills". . . . But she had to settle for second place as Jennie was too well established for too many years as "Queen."

Her one claim to fame was that Jerry Lewis started at her hotel as busboy when Jerry's mother Ray and dad Danny worked there. When I first interviewed Lillian way back when I did research on my first book about the Borscht Belt she resented the fact that I used too many pictures about Grossinger's and not many about Brown's. I explained that the only picture she offered me was one of Jerry Lewis, but Jennie had given me access to all her rare collections of pictures with many stars.

Suffice to say that she was envious of Jennie's reputation and her one ambition was to some day present a Big Name that would outshine any star ever booked by her leading competitors, the Concord and Grossinger's. She finally succeeded and the following story is how it all happened that BOB HOPE appeared at Brown's Hotel on July 22, 1978. I got this story from the man who was responsible for the booking, Steve Sheldon, a producer who now lives in Las Vegas.

Steve Sheldon started as an agent and at one time booked over sixty hotels in the Catskills. When Atlantic City opened, the Catskill Mountains suffered greatly for many customers and guests went to Atlantic City. Steve, who had booked big names for conventions including Bob Hope felt that he should try to grab a big name like Bob in order to boost the morale and popularity of the Catskills. He knew that Lillian Brown's greatest ambition was to book the biggest name in show business and show up her rivals, Grossingers and the Concord. Steve Sheldon had Bob Hope's address and took a wild and crazy chance and called him one day. Luckily he found him at home and made the following pitch to Bob: "Bob, you were once a struggling vaudevilian and know that there are few places left for acts to work nowadays. The Catskills, one of those few places, is hurting now that Atlantic City has opened. It would mean a lot to the hotels and the acts if you would agree to play Brown's Hotel while you are appearing nearby in New Jersey."

Bob politely replied, "Son, I don't think the audience would like me in the Catskills. I am used to playing to a younger audience, colleges and young soldiers and am afraid I wouldn't do well there."

Steve was persistent and in jest said: "Bob, if you would do this for me I would guarantee you all the BAGELS AND LOX you could eat!"

Bob Hope laughed and replied, "Kid, I ate bagels and lox before you were born, in Nate and Al's in Beverly Hills."

Steve replied, "And I would put into your contract that I would personally be there."

"Why?" replied Bob.

"So that I could tell which were the bagels and which was the lox."

Bob laughed out loud and replied, "Kid, I like your chuztpa. I'll do it if I get my price."

He quoted his figure and Steve said okay without even asking the Browns, for he knew they would never say no to the greatest star ever to play the Catskills.

So on July 22, 1978, Bob Hope appeared at Brown's Hotel and made Catskill history. He told me that he never made one cent on this booking but did it so that, as he put it, he could "repay the Catskills for giving me my first start . . . and repaying my roots."

SUMMARY

I keep wondering what there was about the Borscht Belt that manufactured so many big theatrical names. They all had BORSCHT IN THEIR BLOOD. What kind of food did they have that brought out a Van Johnson, an Earl Wrightson, a Gene Barry, a John Garfield, a Shelley Winters? What kind of air did they breathe at Swan Lake that turned erstwhile violin players Henny Youngman and Jan Peerce into stars? What kind of water did Sid Caesar, Phil Silvers, and Jackie Miles drink that helped to develop their funny bones? What was it that inspired Arthur Kober to write "Having a Wonderful Time" and Herman Wouk to scribble *Marjorie Morningstar*?

The Borscht Belt not only spawned Clifford Odets, Morrie Ryskind, and Yip Harburg, but it also gave birth to Bob Cousy, and it groomed Barney Ross and other top sports figures. Then, too, the hills are filled with the sound of music made by those successful doctors and lawyers who worked their way through college serving as busboys, bellhops, and Romeos to the love-starved file clerks. And for those whose lifelong ambition was matrimony, Mountaindale, Monticello, and South Falls Church proved the greatest Garden of Eden since Eve propositioned Adam.

Chapter 3

My Boss, David N. Katz, of Totem Lodge

*I*first met David N. Katz at his office in Court Street, Brooklyn, in 1927. I was recommended to him by some mutual friends, Charlie and Blanche Alberts, who had watched me entertain at Camp Everett and had told Mr. Katz that I was the man he needed at Totem Lodge. Totem was a new summer adult camp located at Burden Lake in Averill Park, New York, outside Albany, and had become a favorite vacation spot for many young New Yorkers. He asked me to audition at his home on Carroll Street in Brooklyn. He had made a practice of inviting talent to his home to audition for the summer and in this way he had free entertainment for his friends and relatives.

I brought my band with me and of course featured my Russian

hit, "Katinka." That clinched it. I got my first contract for $1,500 for the summer. Moss Hart was then social director at Camp Copake, Max Lieberman at Tamiment, Danny Kaye at White Roe Lake, Ernie Glucksman at Green Mansions, and Dore Schary at Grossinger's. Katz always told me in later years that he had a choice of any one of the others, but chose me. He would say with a twinkle in his eye, "I wonder what happened to the other guys?" Who would ever think that my one rendition of "Katinka" in Katz's house that Sunday would result in a career of almost thirty summers!

I sold him a package deal that summer. I put Jerry Drexler in charge of my band of ten men; Eli Steuer, my assistant; Mischa Auer, my dramatic director; and hired a comedian by the name of Benney Lessey. It was while at Totem Lodge that first year that Benney Lessey and Julie Oshins teamed together and made quite some noise around the nightclub circuit. I also hired a guy by the name of George Tobias as assistant dramatic director. He was riding instructor but had theatrical ambitions and talent. He became one of our prominent Hollywood movie actors.

My formula at Totem that first year was simple. I gave the guests lots of laughs. Corn plus more corn. I kept them busy all day and night. I was a huge success the first year. I had followed a fellow by the name of Sir John Pecora, who had given the Totem guests Gilbert and Sullivan and serious entertainment. They wanted corn, burlesque, and laughs, and I was known as "Corny but commercial Tobias."

With a complete musical comedy staff to work with I thought it would be novel if I presented a complete Broadway musical comedy for the first time in the resort business, and so I chose "Good News" and "Connecticut Yankee" as my first shows. Before the summer, with the help of my wife and friends, I attended several perform-ances of the shows and took lots of notes, worked day and night until I had a condensed version of the shows and all the meat and laughs. Then I got copies of the music from the publishers and had my scenery man copy the scenery sketches from the shows. By the time July came around I was able to reproduce almost in their entirety both shows every two weeks and repeat them in August.

When I look back and think of the trouble we went through just to put on two performances a summer, I can't believe it. We had to rehearse in between keeping our guests happy and busy during the day and putting on evening entertainment of varied sorts.

My Boss, David N. Katz, of Totem Lodge

We only produced two musical comedies a summer and alternated every Saturday with an original revue, which was easier to produce. Much of Max Liebman's "Show of Shows" material was born in this way and kept in the trunk for that important day. Some of the greatest material is still in trunks awaiting an opportunity to be presented.

We did this for many years, producing such Broadway hits as "Hold Everything," "Girl Crazy," "Whoopee," "Rosalie," "Of Thee I Sing," "Roberta," "As Thousands Cheer," "Strike Me Pink," "Anything Goes," "Follies," and many others. We never had any difficulty with producers, insofar as royalties were concerned. They all knew we did not charge admission and used half an amateur cast, so thought no harm done to their box office..

One day Jennie Grossinger decided to try and do likewise. However, instead of copying scripts inconspicuously, she bought up a whole row of orchestra seats for one of George White's "Scandals" and took along a crew of writers and stenographers. You can imagine the commotion they started. When George White found out what was going on, he immediately put a stop to it and advised his attorney to notify me and others to stop all similar plans. That was the end of Broadway musicals in summer resorts without permission of the copyright owners.

Later, professional stock companies, like the Stanley Wolf players, et. al., presented condensed versions of plays and charged a small fee for the use. They presented the entire show with scenery and cast included for as low as $150 a performance, making it cheaper for resort owners to bring in a new show each week and dispose of the expensive large staff who ate them out of house and kitchen.

As social director it was my duty to hire the staff, collect material, plan the daytime activities and night program, emcee, and act in the shows. I also played most of the comedy leads in the musical comedies—"Connecticut Yankee" (Bill Gaxton's part); "Good News" (Jack Haley's part); "Whoopee" (Eddie Cantor's part), etc., etc. In the Eddie Cantor chapter of this book there is the story of how Eddie saved me from some embarrassment when Ziegfeld tried to stop me from presenting my version of "Whoopee" at Totem without his permission.

I suppose it was the borscht in my blood or the opportunity to exploit and use all my talents that made me stick to the Borscht Belt all those years. The programs at night varied and the entire industry took a complete turn several times in three decades.

Owners of resorts are a special brand of people. There are good and bad in every business, but somehow in this business there were mostly bad, with a few exceptions: Harry Scheiner, Walter Jacobs, David Levinson, and Jennie Grossinger. So with apologies to those few good ones, here is a true story of the owner of Totem Lodge.

He was such an unusual character that I had one day hoped to write a book about him, for his life and experiences would make a great book. I think Moss Hart described his experiences with his resort owners in a wonderful manner in his book *Act One,* and Katz was that kind of a man. In order to appreciate his eccentricities, perhaps we should go back to his humble beginnings and how he first got hold of this small resort near Albany and built it up to one of the largest and most reputable summer resorts in the East.

He was born in Europe and came to America in his teens and studied to be a pharmacist. To the end of his days he retained a heavy gutteral Russian accent. He owned a pharmacy in Brooklyn near Eastern Parkway and thrived as the "king of all he surveyed in the neighborhood." He was always destined to be the big man in the neighborhood.

When Prohibition came in he, being in a position to buy alcohol as a druggist, somehow got into the company of a big syndicate of bootleggers. He told us it consisted of some well-known political big shots. He was the fall guy because he furnished the alcohol. When things got too hot, he got out fast, and just in time, with plenty of loot for his efforts.

A friend of his, Dr. George Wolf, a reputable physician in Brooklyn, had bought a small farm outside of Albany on Burden Lake and tried to run a small boarding house there called the Wolf House. He was unsuccessful and was looking for partners or someone to take over. Dave Katz took a liking to this property and with his nephew Louis Sokolow, bought two-thirds interest and decided to develop it as a summer camp for adults. There were few good accommodations, and so to expand, they built tents with wooden floors. He then approached the members of the Tompkins Avenue Boys Association, a well-known men's social club in Brooklyn. He solicited their business and gave them special inducements to spend their vacations at Totem Lodge.

When the single girls heard the place was loaded with men, they flocked to it. He always gave them their money's worth: good food, lousy accommodations, but plenty of fun. That was my department. I kept them busy and happy so that they wouldn't notice or complain about the unsatisfactory rooms.

He was a conniver. His theory was to operate on other people's money. Right from the start, everything he took in went part to him, and the rest to the business, but he made sure he got his first. The method he used in buying and building on credit and peanuts was unbelievable.

Totem was the first adult resort to build a swimming pool, but I know as a matter of fact it was an accident. They needed a warehouse to store some food and merchandise. Mr. Katz figured out a way to get it done for practically nothing. He approached a construction man on a large excavating machine who was working on the county roads near Totem. He asked him if he would like to make a few bucks on his day off. All he had to do was to bring the crane and machine into Totem, dig a large hole behind Burden Hall (one of the buildings), and he would get $25 for his work. The man agreed. On Sunday he rolled the big machine into the camp and went to work on the hole. In an hour he had a large hole dug. Mr. Katz, realizing he was paying for a day's work, told him to dig a larger hole until his day's work was over. He didn't need the hole and didn't know what he would do with it, but it was coming to him and he insisted on getting it. So a tremendous hole was dug behind Burden Hall, and the man with the machine went on his way.

When his partner said, "What are you going to do with the hole?" Dave Katz said, "I've got an idea. We'll build an indoor swimming pool."

"Are you nuts?" said his partner. "This will cost a fortune."

"Not the way I figure it," said Katz.

The next day he went looking through Brooklyn for means and methods. One day he came across a building being demolished alongside Prospect Park—it was the old Brooklyn Athletic Club, or some old bank. He noticed some fine terrazzo marble pieces lying on the sidewalk ready to be taken away and dumped. He asked the foreman if he might take them away and save them the expense. They were glad to get rid of them.

Now he had a tremendous amount of tile and he had to figure out how to get it up to his camp near Albany. He called his friend Sam Rosoff who owned the Hudson River Night Line. Katz had given him business with Totem guests. He asked Sam if he wouldn't mind taking a small load of marble terrazzo up to Albany for him. Sam, thinking it was a small load, readily consented to do him a favor. Katz hired a truck and after five loads, loaded the Hudson River Line so that it keeled over to a dangerous angle. It was too late, and so the boat took it up—for nothing. Another truck and a few dollars and it was in Totem. Now he had to have someone lay this terrazzo for little money to make a pool.

He had contracted for a dance floor and dining room floor made of terrazzo, and he bribed the worker to work overtime and Sundays and holidays and do this special job. So for peanuts, and I do mean peanuts, he finished the first indoor swimming pool in a summer resort. He collected some second-hand stained windows and surrounded the pool, closed it in, and although very few guests used this pool for years, it was a great advertising gimmick.

He used to fool the guests into believing he was going into big construction. When the guests clamored for an outdoor swimming pool, as the walk to the lake down the hill was too steep and inconvenient, he would place some gravel on the spot he chose as a future pool, put a shovel and some tools and a sign, "New Swimming Pool Now Under Construction." He kept this deceit up for years and years. He was an artist when it came to stalling creditors and promoting money. He would go to his season guests during the winter and give them tremendous discounts, up to 50 percent, if they would pay him cash in advance. He would use this money to build and construct and for personal reasons, and of course most of those deals were never recorded on the books and so no tax or government was involved.

As a matter of fact, he even stooped to using the withholding tax from his employees for his own personal or business use, until he owed the government more than fifty thousand dollars. They finally put their foot down and during his last summer in business, the government notified him in mid-August, during the height of the season, that either he pay the money or they would send a marshal in and collect behind the cashier's cage. He pleaded for time. They were adamant. Finally he decided to make a personal plea at the tax department in Albany. He didn't shave for a few days, put on his oldest torn sweaters (which he usually saved for after the summer when the creditors came around), and (I have this from an eyewitness, my brother-in-law, Leonard Streiker, who was his office manager), he made the greatest speech with crocodile tears that under

Hollywood circumstances would have won him an Academy Award. He pleaded for time.

The tax department finally gave him a month and that was all he needed. When the month was up, the season was over, and off he went to Florida where they couldn't find him.

His methods in stalling his creditors were unbelievable. Suffice to say that he went bankrupt two times, and in five years built up an indebtedness to the amount of five hundred thousand dollars. The creditors believed in him and somehow went along with him.

He had a terrific sense of humor, with all his faults; however, he finally got his just rewards. His children turned on him. His son doublecrossed him and with an in-law, Dave Schoenholtz, arranged a bankruptcy with the mortgage owner, who foreclosed on them. They promised to give him his job back and this was an easy method for him to get rid of his debts and start anew. Little did he know they would doublecross him. After they bought the place at mortgage cost, they decided that Katz was a little too hot to continue, and so they reneged on their promise. He threatened to sue, but to no avail. I sued him for my last salary and still have a judgment out against him. There must be a moral to this story someplace. I haven't figured it out yet, except bread cast on the water comes back.

Mr. Katz had many eccentricities. He was of the old school of hotel owners who believed in autocratic rule of his resort. He thought that by putting a fear of the management in his staff they would work harder and toe the mark. Although the pay was small and living conditions for the staff in some cases miserable, he still expected the utmost loyalty from his help.

He started the season off by presenting a long (sometimes three-hour) lecture on the trials and tribulations of a hotel owner and what he expected of his staff. These speeches became so famous because of his "Goldwynism" remarks and the wit and humor interspersed in between his serious remarks that old members of the staff would ask to be invited to attend. Some of the most memorable remarks included: "You notice that we selected the finest boys who are working their way to college from the finest homes. We screened these boys carefully so that we are sure that our lady guests who visit with us will have the company of the finest boys from the finest families in America. It is important for you fellows to mingle with the guests. That is why we allow you to socialize. We have no restrictions as far as our help is concerned. We expect you to come down to the Social Hall after your work, dressed neatly with a tie and jacket and dance with the girls. We even encourage you to romance them, but you should be discreet. Don't forget, President Coolidge goes to bed with his wife but you don't read about it in the morning papers."

In trying to emphasize to the staff that they were entitled to limited freedom, such as all facilities must be available to the "Guests First" (The guest must always come first), but if the facilities were not in use by the guests, Mr. Katz had no objection to the staff using them, he once remarked: "Regarding the use of rowboats, "we have only eighteen rowboats, but we have twenty waiters and busboys. The big problem is: what are we going to do about the other two boys?"

It was very important in those days that the male members of the staff socialize. This was one of the main attractions that would bring the single girls to a resort of this kind—they always knew they could meet a nice single boy working his way through college and perhaps eventually matrimony might result. Let's face it, most single girls went to these kinds of resorts to meet a future husband. So Mr. Katz was very adamant and strict about rules and regulations pertaining to his staff socializing. This was why he hired only college boys in the dining room and sacrificed professional experience for unprofessional help.

However, he made sure the young men were eligible and screened them carefully. He even went to extremes at night to close his gates from eight p.m. until midnight so that the staff wouldn't run out and try to spend the evening in town (Albany). He was so strict that his camp became known among the help as "Katz's Koncentration Kamp."

One staff member, Harry Stockwell, who was the singing tenor and voice of Prince Charming in Walt Disney's first great picture, decided to leave the job because of a better offer. But the question was how to get out of the premises with his trunk without being seen. He waited until midnight one night and, with the help of some of the boys, loaded a rowboat with his trunk and his belongings and rowed across the lake where he had a car and an emissary helped him make a getaway. He knew if he asked Mr. Katz for permission to quit he would be refused, and so he chose this way out.

When the weather was bad, a panic was on at a resort of this kind, for the guests would be thinking of checking out. So Katz had another ruling. When it rained, the staff were not permitted to wear raincoats, hats, or any kind of clothing that would suggest bad weather. His idea was phychologically to try to give the impression that "it never rains at Totem." Can you imagine the staff walking around in the rain without coats or hats and saying to a guest who is soaked, "It's just a slight misty dew, not raining. Just inclement weather. It will clear up any minute." Sometimes this went on for days.

Resort owners were notorious in those days for their convenient bankruptcies and fires. D.N.K. was no exception; he had his share. It was common practice for resort owners who were in financial difficulty to declare 77 B. (Chapter 11) and go into bankruptcy when things were too tough. For instance, when his creditors would squeeze him and threaten him with foreclosure, Katz would threaten to go into bankruptcy and wipe them out. This he did several times, but when things went wrong and he had a rough season, he would always hope for a fire. It was a running gag for me in my weekly tour of the grounds with our guests, pointing out the sights and history. I would always include this surefire gag: "We had a little fire in the Social Hall. The fire was supposed to be after the summer, but something went wrong."

This actually happened. For many years Katz always gagged to his guests that he wished he had a good fire, this would cure all his troubles. One day during September—we were open until the Jewish holidays and the crowd was small—in order to show movies in the large social hall, he installed an old-fashioned cracker barrel stove. We placed it in the middle of the hall on some sheet metal. This heated the hall so that we could show movies and provide entertainment. One night we showed a movie and after the movie all the guests and musicians went up to the lobby of Burden Hall for dancing as it was warmer and cozier. An hour later one of the band members who went down to the hall to pick up some personal belongings ran back shouting, "The hall is on fire." We all rushed down and I, with my undying loyalty and devotion to Totem Lodge, dived under the hall, where the flames were largest, with water buckets and sand. After a long struggle and with the help of others, the fire was put out and we saved the hall. I was congratulated by all for my bravery. When I faced Katz, expecting his thanks, he looked at me disdainfuly and cried, "You and your God-damned loyalty and bravery. I've waited for years for a fire, and you had to put it out." He spit down on the ground in disgust and walked away.

Because of their short season, summer resort owners were regarded as poor credit risks. I have heard of shrewd businessmen who had invented new ways to dodge creditors, but D.N.K. was the master of them all. A merchant knew that if he didn't get paid for his merchandise by August 15 when the season reached its peak, or by Labor Day at the latest, the chances were that he would have to wait until the following year to collect his bill. Some shrewd summer resort owners figured out different ways and means to delay payment so that they could be held over for another year.

D.N.K. was such a master at this art that he piled up a remarkable record of approximately five hundred thousand dollars in debts within the a period of ten years. He depended upon his personal friendship and forceful personality to con his merchants into carrying him over from one year to the next. When the debt grew too large to pay, he would threaten his creditors with bankruptcy and in that way force his creditors into settling accounts from 25 cents to 50 cents on the dollar.

Many of the larger creditors, such as food merchants who sold him as much as $25,000 worth of food for the short three-month summer season, were wise to his methods and went along with him, but made it up in another way. They would pad his bills 10 or 20 percent, or short-weigh his merchandise, knowing he would not object as long as they carried him for another summer, and they made up their losses in that way. He knew he was being cheated by many but he didn't care; as long as he could get his share out of the season's take, he didn't care how much he owed. He was a firm believer in the "O.P.M." system—always use "Other People's Money," or take from Peter to pay Paul. That was his business philosophy. He was one of the few old-fashioned hotel owners who didn't look at the figures and cared even less for percentages or profit-and-loss statements.

With a half-million income each summer, no one could figure out why he couldn't pay off his creditors and leave enough profit for himself. Everyone wondered what happened to the money. There were many reasons and explanations for this. My own analysis was that he lived very high and had tremendous personal expenses bringing up three children, sending two of them through college, launching his oldest son in a medical career. Also, with no other business to support him the rest of the year, he had to live on his summer income.

My Boss, David N. Katz, of Totem Lodge

He could have been a terrific actor but missed his profession. If he had been an actor, he could have been the greatest and probably would have copped an Academy Award somewhere along the line. D.N.K. was a great showman and, I repeat, missed his profession. In those days the guests visiting adult camps of this kind were not too particular with regard to accommodations. They were mostly young single men and women whose main purpose was to have fun, meet some other young people, enjoy good food and fun. D.N.K. gave them the best food available and encouraged the best entertainment. It was my job to keep them happy day and night, and tire them out with activities so that they wouldn't mind sleeping on hard beds: army cots with thin mattresses and army horse-blankets, with only a sink in the room—the bathrooms and showers were in another building (public bath building)—and no hot water except in a central shower room. The roofs of the cottages leaked and the window screens were torn, so that bugs and mosquitoes had a ball.

Leonard Streiker, my brother-in-law, worked for Katz as reservations manager and first assistant for many years. I know he has lots of stories to relate about Katz, but to get him to recall and talk about them is another matter. Following is one story I finally got out of him.

THE STATE TROOPER AND KATZ

We all have heard through other stories what a great con merchant Katz was. As a matter of fact, we have often referred to him as the Jewish Ponzi. (Ponzi was one of the notorious con merchants and swindlers of his time.)

Once Katz was driving his family to Totem on the Old Post Road. He was stopped in Kingston for some minor reason. Katz used his charm and persuasiveness on the state trooper and finally bribed him with a bottle of perfume he had in the car. The trooper finally accepted.

Fade in–Fade out.

Two weeks later Katz was stopped again by the same trooper at the same spot. "What are you, a wise guy or something? Giving me an empty bottle of perfume for my wife?"

"What do you mean, empty?"

"That's what I said. I gave my wife the perfume and when she opened it, it was empty."

Katz, who thought faster than anyone else when in a spot, said, "I guess it evaporated, as many of the finest perfumes do. Here's a bottle of the finest champagne that I happen to have with me. This will make up for the perfume." The state trooper reluctantly accepted the champagne and let Katz go.

Fade in–Fade out. Two weeks later.

Katz passed through Kingston and once again the same trooper stopped him.

"I've been waiting for you, Katz. I guess you think you put it over on me. Well, you won't get away with it."

"What did I do now?"

"Nothing much. Remember that champagne bottle you gave me? Well, when I opened it up it tasted like vinegar."

"Vinegar?" asked Katz in his most disappointed voice. "How could that be? That was the finest Piper Heidsich bottle of champagne. Did you keep it standing up in your ice box?"

"Yes," said the trooper.

"Well, that's the reason—you must put it down on its side. If you stand it up, it will turn sour." He had nothing more to give him so he said, "You know me, I'm Katz. I own that famous resort, Totem Lodge. Why don't you and your wife come up to visit me? We're only one hour away. You'll be my guest for dinner, see the show and have a wonderful time." The trooper decided to accept the invitation and said okay.

As we say in show business—fade in–fade out. Two weeks pass and now it's Labor Day. It's Saturday night of the biggest weekend and Katz gives explicit instructions to his gate police and those in charge of admission not to allow anyone through, not even to contact him if anyone asks for him because everyone in the area knows him and tries to crash the big weekend with choice entertainment. He won't even answer the phone before showtime. It's 8:00 P.M. and the state trooper and his wife arrive at the gate. He asks for Katz, identifies himself, but the guard at the gate and Leonard Streiker (who was there to identify certain visitors and stop others) didn't know the man and refused to call Katz. No matter how much the man pleaded, Leonard refused. In a fit of rage the trooper drove to another town, placed a person-to-person call to

David N. Katz. Katz, thinking it must be urgent, answered the phone, and all he heard at the other end of the line was a rough, loud, screaming voice say: "Don't you ever take Route 9 through Kingston again. . . ."

KATZ AND THE TAXI DRIVER

One day in New York Katz hailed a cab. He and the driver, both talkative people, struck up a conversation. The driver told Katz that his wife was in the hospital. Katz, who happened to be president of the board of directors of one of Brooklyn's leading hospitals, Beth David, asked the driver which hospital his wife was in. The driver said Beth David. "That's funny," said Katz."I happen to be on the board of directors."

The driver answered, "Isn't that a coincidence? I'm not worried, because she's in the hands of a wonderful young doctor who just finished interning."

"What's his name?" asked Katz.

"Dr. Seymour Katz," he answered.

"That's my son."

"Is that so," said the driver, getting a bit doubtful. The cabbie continued talking about his wife, saying, "After she gets out of the hospital I'm planning to take her to a little farm upstate."

"Where?" asked Katz.

"Near Albany."

"I happen to have a hotel near Albany. Where's your place?"

"A little spot near Burden Lake. I always go there so I can sneak over to the big hotel on the other end of the lake and enjoy the shows."

"What's the name of the hotel?" asked Katz, glowingly.

"Totem Lodge."

"I happen to own Totem Lodge. My name is David N. Katz."

The cab driver looked over his shoulder in disgust, pulled the cab over to the sidewalk, opened the back door and yelled at Katz: "Come on. Get the hell out of my cab, you wise guy. What are you, some kind of nut or something?" Katz had to get out of the cab, even though he tried to explain that it was all true and coincidental.

39

MORE BOSS STORIES

Decoration Day weekend of 1940 or '41. We had Joe E. Lewis, Block and Sully, and Harry Hershfield as our stars. They were in the bar and there was a big crowd. Suddenly a little snippy guy, about 25 years old, told everyone he was an MGM scout from Hollywood, dropping names all over the place. Many wise-guy guests accepted his invitation to drink and in one day this scout ran up a tab for $200. Katz was worried and called him into his office the next day. "Look, we don't know you. So you're a big man in Hollywood. I think you ought to give us a down payment as long as your bills are piling up, to show good faith."

He said, "Sure," and wrote out a check for $200.

Katz, who trusted nobody, called the bank. They never heard of the man. In the meantime the tab grew more. Katz brought him in again and told him about his call to the bank.

"Okay," said the guest, "I'll wire my wife for the money." So he wired his wife. The telegram came back through the office girl who showed it to Katz. The wire said, "Drop Dead." Katz called the state police.

So the guest said, "All right. Call my mother, let me speak to her. But when you speak to her, tell her the bills are for $700 instead of $400." (He wanted to make $300 on his mother.)

Katz called the mother. As soon as she heard Totem Lodge, she asked, "How much?" In the meantime, the troopers took his guest to jail.

We were sitting around the office discussing this guest, when another guest told us he knew he was a phony because he went to the "scout's" room and found a pair of shoes with holes in them—my brother is a detective and you can always spot a phony by his shoes. Katz said, "That's a wonderful thing. You're right." And with that he crossed his legs and his shoes showed holes in them.

This will give you another idea of how Katz's mind worked when it came to money. A Brooklyn guy owed Katz $300 and Katz hadn't seen him in a year. One day, by accident, Katz bumped into this guy on the street. They gave each other the big hello and Katz finally got to the point. "By the way, Sammy, last year I gave you $300." Sam said, "It slipped my mind." So Katz said, "Here I am." The fellow answered that he didn't carry $300 with him. Katz said, "So write a check." The other guy, thinking fast, said, "Look, today is Saturday (Shabas), and I'm a religious man. I can't write a check on the sabbath."

Katz said, "Okay, so date it Monday." The guy wrote the check.

JOE THE BELLHOP

The first comedian I ever met was not even a professional. He was an amateur, Joe Tucker, who worked as a bellhop on my staff at Totem Lodge in the early thirties, from 1932–1936. Joe later became a successful liquor salesman connected with Carstairs Company.

In those days the young men who applied for jobs for Totem Lodge were usually college students whose main purpose was to earn enough money during the summer to pay for their college tuition during the winter. Joe Tucker was one such guy, from Brooklyn, working his way through college.

But he was different from the rest. When he walked into our New York Totem office on the corner of 42nd Street and Broadway, he was not scared like the other applicants. Katz would brook fear into all the boys with his Hitler-like interviews. Joe didn't scare easily. As a matter of fact he was very arrogant, independent and very funny. He walked in brazenly and said to me, sitting in the front office, "I want to see the boss."

I replied, "Have you an appointment?"

He answered, "I don't need an appointment; he needs me." His frank reply shocked me into ushering him into the boss's office. Here was the way the interview ran:

KATZ: What can I do for you, young man?
JOE: I'm looking for a job at Totem for the summer.
KATZ: What kind of a job?
JOE: Anything. (When a young man asks for any kind of job, look out. He evidently has no talent whatsoever. Katz, intrigued by his frankness and overconfidence, thought he would rib Joe, and continued:)
KATZ: Do you think you could handle the manager's job?
JOE: Yes, I think so.
KATZ: I'm sorry, but the manager's job is taken.
JOE: How about the social director?

KATZ: Sorry, but Tobias has been with us for five years.
JOE: Have you hired the head waiter?
KATZ: Yes, that position is filled.
JOE: How about captain in the dining room?
KATZ: I'm sorry, that's filled too.
JOE: Then I'll take a waiter or busboy's job—they make good money.
KATZ: I'm sorry. The only jobs open are for caddies and bellhops.
JOE: Which make more money?
KATZ: A bellhop if he's good.
JOE: I'll take it.

And so Joe became a bellhop, but not the usual kind. It was immediately noticeable that Joe was an unusual guy with a tremendous sense of humor—insult humor—but he would insult in such a manner that you never felt disturbed or insulted. When a bellhop insults you, you realize at once that it must be a gag and so we all went along with the gag. Even the boss, who was very strict with his help, had a great sense of humor and went along with Joe and his comedy routines.

When a guest checked in, the first shock he got when Joe took care of him was to hear Joe remark: "Pick up your bag and follow me." Of course everyone in the office would laugh and the guest would join in the laughter, foolishly picking up his bag and following Joe. Joe would give a running description of the camp, its faults, defects, bad points, and would throw in gags all the way. By the time the guest reached the bungalow he was laughing so much that Joe invariably wound up with tips twice as large as the other bellhops.

Some of the running gags that Joe used on the guests even before they reached their rooms might have been lifted from Henny Youngman or others, or Youngman might have lifted his from Joe Tucker. I never did find out but they have been kicked around a lot since then.

When a guest asked him "Is this hotel fireproof?", he would reply: "Only during the season. We had a fire last week but that was a mistake. The fire was supposed to be *after* Labor Day."
GUEST: "How are the girls up here?"
JOE: "Well, to give you an idea, see that horn on the Totem pole? It only blows when a virgin passes, and it hasn't blown in ten years."

My Boss, David N. Katz, of Totem Lodge

When he finally brought the guest to his room, he made fun of the room, which was a reverse switch and very effective, as the accommodations were very bad. He pulled gags like: "The only reason this room has a door is to hold up the walls," or, "This room is very clean. They change the bed sheets every day, from bed to bed."

"The service in this joint is wonderful. You press a button, the dresser comes out. Press another button, the radio comes out. Press another button, the chambermaid comes out. Press the chambermaid, your teeth come out."

Another favorite stunt of Joe Tucker's was that if a guest checked in with a heavy trunk (too heavy for Joe), he would hire a kitchen porter for 50 cents and charge the guest a dollar for bringing the trunk to the room.

Joe's insult humor was best when I called on him to entertain in our Wednesday night vaudeville shows presenting both guests and staff. Knowing Katz's reputation as a hard, shrewd, and tough boss, Joe had by now established himself as a comedy bellhop, used the boss as his subject and got a big laugh from the audience, and also got laughs from the boss. Naturally, all the staff would wait and watch Katz's reactions to Joe's insults, expecting him to run up on the stage, pull Joe off and fire him on the spot. Instead, Katz, wise with the ways of guests and believing at all times that the guest is always right, went along with the insults and laughed louder than anyone in the audience. Of course the rest of the staff joined in with the laughs.

Some of the best insult gags about Katz were:

"Mr. Katz is a very conservative guy. When he goes to the dog races he bets two dollars on the rabbit, to show."

"In a poker game when he bets, you could throw away four kings."

"He has an even disposition—miserable all the time."

"When I first went to see him about a job I told him I could sing, dance, play the piano, put on shows, write and tell jokes. He replied, 'That's good, and so it shouldn't be a total loss, you could be a bellhop too.'"

"When I wanted to warm up to him I would say, 'We're having nice weather.' He answered, 'Since when are we partners? I'm having nice weather.'"

I PLAYED THE PIANO
IN A WHOREHOUSE

When Jack Benny invited former President Harry Truman to appear on his TV show to play the piano, Mr. Truman politely refused, remarking, "My only ambition as a musician was to play the piano in a whorehouse." I had that experience in the '30s, but it was not as wicked as it sounds.

It was during one of my many summers as Entertainment Director at Totem Lodge. One of the unforgettable characters who worked on our staff was Joe Tucker, who was a combination of bellboy, comedian, and general popular personality. He had many sideline rackets, such as director of service and any other sideline where he could make a buck. One of his specialties was arranging for visits to the neighboring whorehouse in Troy, N.Y.

During one summer one of the victims of his heckling around the camp and on the stage was a timid soul who played the piano in the orchestra. His name, for want of a better one, was Sidney Fink. Although this sounds impossible, and strange as it seems, Sidney admitted to being a virgin—at the age of 28. A musician at that age to be a virgin was an unknown oddity.

Joe Tucker took advantage of Sidney's weakness and started a vicious campaign among the male guests, who worked on Sidney and convinced him that he could get rid of his nervousness and pimples if he would visit Troy. The lovable humorist, Harry Hershfield, was one of our guests, and when he finally convinced Sidney to go to Troy, he arranged a safari of male guests to accompany Sidney. They asked me, as Entertainment Director, to go along. I explained that I was a married man with a reputation to uphold, but they finally got my wife's permission with the promise that they would make sure I wouldn't go upstairs and take an active part.

The safari landed at one of Troy's famous spots (Joe had arranged for the party). We were received royally and Sidney had the pick of the crop. I was induced to sit down and play the piano while Sidney went upstairs among the cheers and encouragement of all the guests (there were a dozen of us). I played the piano, with the proper musical selections, while we all enjoyed a sing-along and waited patiently. Finally the big moment came—Sidney was through. As he walked down the stairs with a smile on his face, we all cheered and sang, "He's a Jolly Good Fellow." That's all there was to it. So I really and honestly can brag that I PLAYED PIANO IN A WHOREHOUSE.

Chapter 4

Sex Takes a Holiday

Sex is the number one activity around the world, but particularly in the resort business. It is only natural that once a boy or girl, man or woman goes on vacation, all let their cares go to pot and their hearts go to anyone who'll have it. We have gone into the subject quite a lot with many stories of Boy Meets Girl. Moss Hart describes so vividly his experiences as a social director when he had to cater to, dance with, and sleep with those so-called wall flowers, sometimes known as "Pots," "Dogs," "Carlottas," "Shirleys," or anything you might care to call them.

We've heard the stories of the young girls who, finding it difficult to compete with other guests because of looks or other fallacies, would fall back on the staff, the musicians, the social director, the artists, the waiters, busboys, bellhops, or anyone working at the hotel. Without romance the vacation would be a flop, or as Mother would say in Jewish, "In Dred Der Gelt." (Money goes to hell.)

The girls would sacrifice their sunshine, sunburn, tennis, boat-

47

ing, swimming, and other athletic facilities to hang around the social hall during rehearsals so that they could get better acquainted with the staff. Or many a girl came home with a pale white face because she spent most of her time in the dining room helping her boyfriend set up the tables or wash the dishes in the kitchen. How many times did you see that lovelorn girl sitting in the office next to her bellhop friend to keep him company? The boss was afraid to throw her out or fire the bellhop for fear he would lose a customer.

I guess the girls fell for staff for other reasons too. They were mostly their own age, unattached, free lovers, wild thinkers, willing givers, and could be trusted. Somehow or other a girl thought that professional performers would never "kiss and tell." They were discreet, they had to be.

There was the story of Harry Spear who met the fancy of the owner's wife and was chased out of the building with a butcher knife. And how Lou Saxon fell for a mobster's moll and was taken for a ride eight miles from the hotel and dumped, stripped naked, to walk home alone.

Although told many times by many people in many forms, this is a true story at Totem Lodge. Somehow the riding master, like the camp artist, was always considered the most romantic type. Maybe it was because in those old days movie stars wore riding boots and habits as did Hollywood directors. I don't know what it was, but one summer the riding master, let's call him Sam, was truly a lady's man. One day up in the children's playground, where the children were kept fenced into their own area away from their parents, and guided by counselors, one kid was bragging about how well he knew the riding master. To a kid, the riding master was a god. The other kid said he knew him even better because he let him ride a pony every day at the stable. The third kid looked down at the others and bragged: "That's nothing, the riding master sleeps with my Mommy every night when my Daddy is away."

When the counselors heard this, you can imagine the excitement and gossip. It soon became the number one topic in camp—everyone knew but the two involved (which is often the case). It was fun watching the two make those secret rendezvous around the bar at the social hall. They would start at opposite ends as though they never knew each other and gradually move over to the center of the bar, where they would whisper sweet nothings in each other's ear. Then when the show or movie would start, and the lights went out, you could see two shadows (first him, then her) quietly sneak out of the social hall for their secret rendezvous. I guess the husband never found out.

Then there is another true story about the musician who had an affair with one of the season guest's wives. Some guests would stay for the entire season, and their husbands would come only on weekends. Some of the wives found the middle of the week the right time for extra romance and usually with the musicians (who were more mature and discreet). This particular musician was truly knocked out from his lovemaking all week. The husband, upon his return, hearing of all the attention paid his wife by the musician, was actually so naive that he thanked him profusely for keeping his wife company, and to show his appreciation, took the musician into a Troy whorehouse, but he had no strength left to enjoy it.

Then there were the women (sometimes married, sometimes single) who somehow worshiped and glorified the actors, social directors, singers, dancers—anyone in show business. It was a glamorous business and attracted many outsiders, even as it does today. The wife or guest would volunteer to take part in the show so that she could have companionship and get better acquainted with any one of the staff that she particularly liked. It didn't matter if the talent was not there as long as she could be around show people, who were always known as "fun" people. She would rather help the artist paint scenery, or sit for a painting (sometimes nude) than go out and ride a horse, play tennis, or swim in the lake, or go for a hike. Here at least she could get some romance, and without romance, as we said before, "In Dred Der Gelt."

There was a beautiful model by the name of Helen, who had just lost her young husband by some tragic early death. It just happened that she came to Totem to forget her sorrow and when she saw me, she almost fainted. It seemed by a strange coincidence that I looked and acted very much like her late husband, who was also in show business. That's all I needed—me, a married and true-blue character who had enough trouble keeping the girls away, because they all flocked to the social director, particularly if he could play the piano, sing, and write songs. This girl hung on to me like there was no tomorrow, and I had alot of difficulty losing her with my wife and daughter around. Believe it or not, I held off her advances. It was a tough fight, Mom, but I won (???????).

Then there was the married woman who wrote lyrics (everyone is a songwriter). Strange as it seems, some of her lyrics were worthy of publication. Being a guy who is always looking for a good idea for

my tunes, I encouraged her writing and finally succeeded in getting
a few songs published with her. She encouraged and tried romance,
but once again (believe it or not), I fought it off. Luckily, she lives
out of town.

JACK SOBLE was an artist hired by me to paint scenery. As a
sideline he was allowed to make portrait paintings of guests. Somehow or other an artist was always considered a free thinker and a
free lover. So whenever a female guest, whether single or married,
wanted a little romance or sex, she was sure to get it with the artist,
and she also was sure he would be discreet and could be trusted not
to talk.

Jack painted the scenery and in order to facilitate matters and be
close to his stage and insure some privacy, he built a room over the
social hall stage at Totem. You had to walk up about ten steps on a
narrow stairway to reach the room. There were two windows leading out to the woods, with no chance of Peeping Toms, and the roof
of the social hall and stage was the roof of the studio (he called it a
studio to give it class, mystery, and romance). When it came to sex,
he was the pro of them all and the busiest guy in town. In order to
keep the snoopers away, once he placed a pipe on the railing of the
staircase (it was a cruise ladder with side arms) and had the electrician wire the pipe with electricity. Then he would put the switch on
when he didn't want to be disturbed and no visitors would dare walk
up or they would get a 220 volt shock that would knock them off the
stairs.

He used to display his paintings and, of course, invite the girls up
to look at his etchings. There was always one painting upside down.
We never could figure that out until he finally confessed that this
painting was for the girl, to keep her company and let her enjoy a
painting while lying on his bed, with him usually on top.

Here's another true sex story. Unbelievable, but nevertheless
true. It it similar to the one about the sax player, but this time it
truly happened to the drummer. Let's call him Phil (because that
was his real name.) He had a hot romance going with a doctor's wife
who spent the entire summer at Totem Lodge. She was a
nymphomaniac and certainly was not satisfied by the weekend
visits of her stately, dignified, and naive husband. The romance was
going stronger and stronger all summer until everyone in the camp
knew about it but the husband, as usual. This turned out to be not
only a summer romance, but the oversexed wife, realizing what she

had missed all during her married life, decided to leave her doctor husband with the hopes that she might grab the drummer if she were free. Finally came Labor Day, and the big showdown. The wife decided to wait until she got home to break the news to Daddy (doctor husband). Instead of going to pieces or breaking up when she told him, he, like the methodical conservative, dignified doctor he was, decided that he would have a talk with Phil, the drummer, to see if he could salvage his marriage. Sure enough, he went to Phil's house without an appointment and instead of the infuriated husband walking in to kill the lover, the doctor, in a gentlemanly manner, confided in Phil and asked his advice. He told him he knew of the hot romance, his wife had confessed and that she wanted to leave him. Being a good friend of both the doctor and wife, he asked Phil for his advice.

Phil, not wanting to insult the man, and honestly trying to tell him the facts of life, told him that his wife was oversexed, she was lonely, she needed more love, that he was neglecting her, in New York and away, and that she finally decided that sex was more important than respectability as a doctor's wife. He suggested that perhaps the doctor could win her back with more attention and love.

The doctor was very appreciative and gracious and after getting this advice, unconsciously said to Phil, "What do I owe you for this visit?"

The following incident actually took place at Totem Lodge. It is similar to the gag Henny Youngman pulled on some other comedian in the Borscht Belt. After passing along word that there was a beautiful sexy blonde waiting for this comedian in an empty room, when he rushed up he found Henny Youngman dressed as a girl lying in bed. Or, once they brought a cow into the room. . . .

Another time at Totem the gang decided to play a practical joke on two of the guests. They sent word that two professional prostitutes from Troy were waiting down in the empty barber shop (it was June before the barber shop opened, and there was a cot where the barber slept, always in the shop). A few of the staff were let in on the gag and hid behind the social hall, where they could not be seen and still see what was going on in the barber shop.

Sure enough the two guests slowly and quietly walked down the social hall during that evening. (The hall was closed during June). They noticed the barber shop was dark. They knocked at the door and not hearing an answer, walked inside. They groped around the dark room and just as they got inside, Mischa rushed out, knocked heavily at the door, opened the door, in the dark, and screamed, "So you're the guys who've been fooling around with my wife." And he shot off his blank gun (stage gun) in the dark. You never saw two guys run so fast in all your life.

Chapter 5

Borscht Circuit Goes South

Whereas I was hired as program and entertainment director of the Eden Roc Hotel in Florida the winter of 1959 by Harry Mufson, he had hired the cream of the crop of hotel executives on Miami Beach. George Fox was the manager, Sol Geltman in charge of food and catering, Mal Malkin, musical director, and myself. We were proud to be a part of the second-best million-dollar luxury hotel on the beach and Harry Mufson's main goal was to take the spotlight away from his biggest competitor, Ben Novack of the Fountainbleau, who had been the number one hotel owner on the beach for many years.

After the first year at the Eden Roc we had read and heard that Sam Friedlander, owner of the Food Fair chain of grocery stores, was building a bigger and better hotel north of Miami Beach in Hollywood, Florida. A cement strike had delayed his building one year but now it was rumored that he was ready to open his new posh hotel, the Diplomat Hotel, the following winter. It was not a big surprise that all the top executives were approached by Sam with offers that we could not refuse. And so all of us, George Fox, Sol Geltman, Mal Malkin, and I, found ourselves working for Sam Friedlander at the Diplomat Hotel in Hollywood the winter of 1960.

There were now three big hotels: Fountainbleau, Eden Roc, and Diplomat, each one competing for the best talent. Ben Novack had already grabbed Frank Sinatra and his rat pack: Dean Martin, Sammy Davis, Jr., Peter Lawford, and Joey Bishop; and had also presented such top names as George Jessel, Henny Youngman, and many others.

Now it was Eden Roc's turn to grab the headliners. First Harry Belafonte, then Lena Horne, Nat King Cole, Myron Cohen, Joe E. Lewis, Milton Berle, Jane Frohman, and others.

Finally, when the Diplomat opened in Hollywood, Florida, the competition for big names became intense and for some time to this day, almost every big name in show business played one or more of the big three hotels. Here are a few of the most memorable anecdotes.

FRANK SINATRA

If you ask any songwriter who the best male singer in the music business is (through the years), the majority would agree on Frank Sinatra. I know when I appear on TV and radio and am asked the usual question, "Who would you rather have sing or record your songs than anyone else?" I reply without hesitation, "Frank Sinatra." Strange as it might seem, through the years that I have known Frank, he never did record any of my songs, although he told me many times he loved "Miss You" and would someday record it. The closest I came to that hope and dream was a few years ago when Gordon Jenkins, one of Frank's favorite arrangers and musical directors, told me that Frank asked him to prepare an arrangement of "Miss You" for his next session. Unfortunately for me, he never did record it, but I am still hoping.

I first met Frank when he was a skinny little kid singing with Harry James and later with Tommy Dorsey. During my usual rounds of the orchestra leaders trying to get plugs for whomever I was working for or whichever song I was plugging at the time, it was my duty to visit the Meadowbrook Dance Hall in New Jersey and later the Pennsylvania Grill. Frank would always come over to the publisher's table and was a very friendly and warm guy at that time. As years went by, Frank became tougher to approach and harder to talk to. Every time I met him I would say "Hi, Frank," and he'd reply, "Hi." To make sure he remembered me I would reply, "Remember me, Henry Tobias?" He would always reply, "Sure," and go into the first few bars of "Miss you, since you went away dear."

I got to know him better when he appeared with his famous "Rat Pack" at the Fountainbleau Hotel in Miami Beach, Florida, during the winters of 1961 and 1962 with Dean Martin, Peter Lawford, and Joey Bishop. Those days were wild ones for Frank. Some nights they would go out on the balconies and shoot off fire crackers after the show.

Some nights during their performance, Sammy Davis, Jr., interrupted their act by running on stage to ad lib with them, despite the objections of his Eden Roc boss, Harry Mufson, who was Ben Novack's bitter competitor. Those were the nights when all hell broke loose on the stage of the Fountainbleau Hotel. As master of ceremonies at the Fountainbleau I was warned by Frank's manager to introduce Frank with only five words: "Ladies and gentlemen, Frank Sinatra."

When I first introduced him on opening night, I began with my usual introduction, "Good evening ladies and gentlemen, this is Henry Tobias, welcoming you to the Fountainbleau Hotel. Here is the star of our show, Frank Sinatra." Frank was about to go on. He stopped dead in his tracks before walking on stage and looking at me the way only Sinatra can look when he's angry, said softly, "Don't you ever do that again."

The next year he appeared at the same hotel. Pat Henry was his pal and the comedian who always opened the show for Frank. As master of ceremonies it was my job to give the signal to Pat when Frank arrived. Usually his manager would cue me when Frank came into his dressing room off the stage entrance and give me the warning. I in turn would give Pat Henry the signal to cut, and Pat understood wherever he was or whatever joke he was saying, that was it. He would exit fast and I would simply announce backstage, "Ladies and gentlemen, Frank Sinatra." I would announce from stage right backstage and Frank would come out stage left. I therefore never saw him during his two weeks' engagement and he never saw me either. One day while walking through the lobby with his entourage, he recognized me and yelled, "Hi Henry, what are you doing here?" I replied with a smile, "I'm the guy who has been introducing you for two weeks." He just laughed and as he walked away started singing, "Miss you, since you went away dear."

NAT KING COLE

One of the most memorable events of my life was when I attended the funeral service for Nat King Cole at the church on Hollywood Boulevard in Hollywood, California. The church was jammed to capacity and overflowing with friends and Nat's music fans, standing outside of the church and on the street, for everyone loved Nat King Cole. My brother Harry first met him when he was playing with a trio at a small club in Hollywood long before he became famous. He asked Nat if he would make a few demos for him with his trio. Nat needed the money and was glad to oblige.

I got to know him better when he was booked into the Eden Roc Hotel during the winter of 1959 where I was working as emcee and entertainment director. Harry Belafonte was the first black entertainer who was allowed to live at a luxurious hotel on the beach. Nat King Cole was the next, but when he learned that only he could live at the Eden Roc and his band had to live at a black hotel in Miami City proper, he said "Thank you, Mr. Mufson, but I would rather live with my band." He used his penthouse suite only for dressing purposes and in between supper and late shows.

The lush Pompeii Room of the Eden Roc Hotel presented two acts—the star of the show and a supporting act. If the star was a singer, the supporting act was a comedian. This time the supporting act was Jack E. Leonard. Fat Jack, as he was affectionately called by other performers, had been ill for a few months and lost a lot of weight. This was his first show since then. Those of you who remember Jack will recall that he was one of the first insult comedians. (He always resented Don Rickles for he claimed that Don stole his act.) On opening night he was told to do no more than thirty minutes, which was the usual time set aside for supporting acts. The star had to do one hour, or thereabouts.

The club was packed as it usually was when any headliner like Nat King Cole opened. Many celebrities were in the audience, including Walter Winchell and the press; many hotel owners, including my future boss, owner of the Fountainbleau Hotel, Ben Novack. When Jack Leonard started, everyone could see that he was not his old self due to his long layoff. He was not getting the usual laughs from his insults and the longer he continued, the more he sweated. It was what we call "Flop Sweat." He insulted everyone in the audience who was well known and loved, including the owner, Harry Mufson. Instead of shortening his act, he kept going on and on beyond his limited twenty to thirty minutes.

I kept watching Nat King Cole backstage. He was smoking cigarette after cigarette and didn't mumble one word, but you could see that he was getting restless, for he knew that the opening act is there to warm the audience up and they were getting colder and colder.

Soon I got a message from the owner out front to get him off, no matter how. He was laying his biggest egg. The stage was a very large one and could move up and down. I tried signaling to him to cut with the usual sign across my neck. He kept going and dying and going and dying. Finally the boss himself came back and said,"Tobias, if you don't get him off right away, you're fired!"

I finally gave the order to flash the lights off and on and was about to push the stage down after forty-five minutes, when Jack finally came off stage fuming and cursing the audience, and started yelling at me for trying to cut him. There was no use trying to calm him down, so I went back into the audience where the boss was sitting at a table with Joe E. Lewis, who had just closed the night before. The boss was burning and told me to let him go at once. Joe E. Lewis said, "Harry, you can't do that to Jackie, it would ruin his career. He hasn't been well and his timing was off."

Mufson said to me, "Okay, but cut his act to fifteen minutes, and tell him that's final from me." I spent the next few days and nights fighting and arguing with Jackie until after the third night I had him down to almost fifteen minutes. For years later he blamed me for that unforgettable night when he flopped. I tried to explain that it was the boss's orders and I had no alternative. For years, every time I walked into Lindy's and he was there, he would not speak to me and turned his head away.

HARRY BELAFONTE

I had been hired as program director and master of ceremonies at the Eden Roc Hotel starting December 1957 through 1958, and the first artist to open the famous and beautiful Pompeii Room was Harry Belafonte. He had not reached the top of his career yet but was well on his way. His salary was only five thousand a week, with an option for another twenty-five thousand the next season. To give you an idea of his meteoric rise, two years later the Eden Roc paid Belafonte $25,000 per week.

He was truly a great artist and perfectionist. We won't talk of his artistry for this is too well known. Suffice to say he is the only artist I ever saw who could hold a New Year's Eve audience (after midnight, when they were all drunk) spellbound. I had seen many stars flop on New Year's Eve because it is almost impossible to keep an audience quiet after the old year goes out and the new year is welcomed in. I bet Harry a small wager he couldn't keep them quiet. He said, "It's a bet, watch me." And darned if he didn't go on that stage a quarter after midnight and you could have heard a pin drop.

He was and still is a dedicated man and highly sensitive: dedicated to the great cause of integration and highly sensitive to the fact that he was the first Black performer allowed to stay at a beach hotel. It was the owner, Harry Mufson, who first broke that barrier. However, knowing how ticklish this problem was in the South, you would expect an intelligent star of his stature to be very careful and not look for incidents. He was unafraid. Against everyone's advice he volunteered to sing the Star Spangled Banner at the Orange Bowl football game on New Year's Day. He was warned there might be reprisals, and there were, but he sang above the noise and objections, and lost his voice. We had to substitute Myron Cohen for his evening performance.

I was a nervous emcee who worried about everything, and everyone, and it was my job to see that the performers were backstage and ready in plenty of time. Harry Belafonte knew this and always teased me. I would call him at his room and tell him it was a half hour before show time, then call again at fifteen minutes; five minutes before show time he still wasn't backstage, and I used to sweat a lot worrying how I could go out and introduce him. The room was always packed. The dance team only went on for ten minutes, and then I had to step out and say, "Ladies and Gentlemen, the star of our show, Harry Belafonte." But what a feeling to go out and wonder if he was ready. Just a minute before stage time he would appear and smirkingly look at me and say, "Had you worried, didn't I?"

This kept up all during the engagement. When I complained to the management they simply laughed, for the star can do no wrong.

If anyone could get ulcers from worrying, this was the way to do it. He thought he gave them to me, but it was my nervous nature that acted up, and no ulcers. However when Arnold Shaw wrote an unauthorized biography of Belafonte, he mentioned this incident and said that it gave me ulcers. When Belafonte later appeared at the Fontainbleau Hotel at a benefit for the blind, he met me in the lobby and said, "Hello Henry, how are your ulcers?" I knew what he meant.

Another incident that almost started a race riot was when the Horse Owners of the South, an elite group of Southern gentlemen who owned horses, and their gracious ladies held a benefit at the Pompeii Room with Belafonte as the star. He had a habit of singing directly to the ladies, stepping up close to the front of the stairs with his tight pants, and looking down into their bare bosoms. He reeked with sex, and that's why he was such a big favorite with the women. This night he looked too close and too long and a drunken man stood up with a bottle in his hand and was ready to let go, when fortunately some other fellows stopped him in time. That was one time I thought there would be a race riot in the room that would long be remembered.

ELVIS PRESLEY

The year was 1961. I was entertainment director at the fabulous Fountainbleau Hotel in Florida. Elvis Presley had just been released from the Army and was making his first television special to be taped at the Fountainbleau. Colonel Parker was well known for his flamboyant and unusual eccentricities. He insisted that free tickets be given only to teenagers and boys and girls who bought Presley records, and his fans. When my boss, Ben Novack, found this out, he told me to go to the Presley suite and insist that Colonel Parker give him one hundred tickets to be distributed to the Fountainbleau guests only. Said Ben, "After all, I am giving him a suite of rooms, the entire top floor, paying for all the facilities in the ballroom for his broadcast. The least he can do is invite some of my guests."

I went directly up to the top floor where Colonel Parker had reserved an entire floor for Elvis and his entourage. When I stepped off the elevator I was seized by two strong-armed men who searched me carefully. I tried to explain to the men that I was the entertainment director here at the hotel and that my boss, the owner, had asked me to see the Colonel and demand a hundred tickets for the TV show. They wouldn't listen but hustled me into another room where some stranger sat at a desk and started asking me questions.

I again tried to explain why I was there. This time I was getting pretty mad and started to shout. Suddenly from out of the next room came an old friend of mine, Paul Case. He looked at me and started to laugh and the rest of the boys in the room joined in the laughter. "What the hell is this all about?" I screamed at Paul. He couldn't stop laughing, but finally admitted that the colonel decided to play a joke on me and give me the works, not only for laughs but to show how carefully he guarded his prize possession, Elvis Presley. I finally got to see the colonel, who also couldn't stop laughing. He gave me the tickets and every time we meet he still laughs about the incident. Incidentally, he showed his regrets by introducing me to Elvis, who I found to be a very polite and interesting young man.

JOE E. LEWIS

I first met this lovable pixie way back in the late twenties. I was still in my teens around 1924 and 1925, and I used to visit a clubhouse every Sunday in Harlem near 116th Street. The club was called The Regents. In those days there were neighborhood clubhouses such as Prospect Avenue Boys, Tompkins Avenue Boys, etc. They had informal entertainment. The most popular of all the entertainers then was Lovable Joe E. Lewis. This was before he left for Chicago and had his experiences with gangsters. He used to sing my brother's songs and we became friendly.

I followed his career for many years but it wasn't until Joe E. Lewis played the Eden Roc Hotel in 1959–1960 that I got to see him often and get close to him. I was program director and master of ceremonies at the Eden Roc in Miami Beach, Florida, and Joe E. was the headliner. He was notorious for his heavy drinking, which somehow never seemed to interfere with his wonderful performance. However, it worried his close friends Swifty Morgan and his attorney and best pal from Chicago, Judge Abe Marovitz. Before the opening night they came to me and asked if I wouldn't act as chaperone for Joe E. All I had to do was stay with him and try to keep his friends from buying him drinks so that he might be sober for his first performance. You could never let Joe E. know this for he would be insulted and provoked, so it had to be done tactfully.

I succeeded before the first show, but in between the first and second shows, Harry Mufson, the owner, gave Joe E. Lewis a big opening night party. As the guest of honor, he had to drink with everyone. I failed in my second attempt. I have seen Joe E. perform under the influence of liquor but never have I seen him actually being carried on the stage and despite his condition, remember his lines and songs. Of course this was mostly due to the brilliant work of his accompanist, Austin Mack, who knew how to cue Joe E. when he fumbled his opening lines. He was the most lovable comedian in the business.

JOEL GREY

Everyone knows that Joel Grey was the son of the once-famous orchestra leader and recording artist, my good friend Mickey Katz. Mickey had made his reputation on radio and records back in the forties and fifties with his delightful Jewish renditions of popular song hits of the day such as "Mule Train" and others. His records on the Capitol label sold millions and he was a big favorite on radio, especially to the Jewish people who loved his homespun humor and music. I remember when I used to visit my folks in California every winter, came Sunday morning, Mother would stop everything or anything she was doing and make us all listen, as her Michele, as she lovingly called him, was on the air.

When I traveled with Eddie Cantor as pianist and writer, we played Miami Beach to do a benefit for the Red Cross. This was one of the many charitable benefits Eddie played in which one pint of blood donated to the Red Cross was charged as free admission to his concert. My wife had not been well and Eddie graciously invited her to come along with him and Ida to Florida for a week's vacation during his engagement.

One day Eddie said, "I understand that Mickey Katz's son Joel is appearing with him in his show "Borschtcapades" in a theatre on Washington Street. I hear he is quite a talent. Let's invite Jennie Grossinger and go to see him." I arranged the party with Jennie and together we went to Lou Brandt's Theatre on Washington Street below Lincoln Road. The show was the usual entertaining vaudeville show that Mickey Katz and Hal Zeigler had been presenting successfully every year in such densely Jewish populated cities as New York, Chicago, Cleveland, Boston, Philadelphia, and Miami.

Joel was not even sixteen years old at that time. He was undoubtedly the hit of the show with his Danny Kaye impression of the song "RUMANIA." Eddie was very impressed and talked about putting him on his radio show or TV at that time, but nothing came of it. However, the next year Hal Zeigler, who had signed Joel to his first managerial contract, asked me if I would write some special material for his act which he was breaking in at the Morocco Club in Montreal, Canada. I agreed to fly to Montreal to see what I could do for him.

After watching Joel's act, I told Hal Zeigler that I couldn't think of anything worthwhile to write for the act. You see, he was just starting and couldn't make up his mind what style act he would do. He was good at everything. He sounded like Danny Kaye when he sang "RUMANIA," Eddie Cantor when he sang comedy songs, and Fred Astaire when he danced. He was a most talented youngster and although I could not write anything for him, Eddie Cantor and I both recognized his great talent and predicted stardom for him.

When I returned to New York, I gave Hal Zeigler my expense bill for the trip to Montreal. It included plane fare, hotel, food, and "late bite," which of course was expenses for exactly what it sounded like, food for a late bite. But Hal Zeigler suspected that "late bite" meant a visit to one of Montreal's famous whorehouses, and to this day whenever I meet Hal, who incidentally became a rich man producing the road companies of "Jesus Christ Superstar," he greets me with the gag, "How is my 'late bite' friend."

The next time I met Joel he was the supporting act at the Diplomat Hotel where I was entertainment director in Hollywood, Florida, during the winter of 1960–61. It was the first big nightclub engagement he had ever played and he was scared. Besides, his wife was about to give birth to their first child and he was worried. It was the policy of the hotel to give first-class accommodations to the stars but the supporting act was usually housed in an adjoining hotel away from the main house. Because of his wife's condition and because we were old friends, I prevailed upon the managing director, George Fox, to allow him to live at the hotel.

A few days before the end of his two-week engagement, his wife had a miscarriage and Joel had to return to his home in California. There was no time to fill in with any other act, so I talked the management into letting me do my act as a fill-in for a few days, and so indirectly Joel was responsible for my getting my first big opportunity to appear with my "Then I Wrote" act in a major important nightclub.

JANE FROHMAN

Jane Frohman was the most publicized and unusual singing star of them all. She had been a singing star of stage and screen for many years and after her near-death airplane crash, she had to go through many operations to survive. Each operation had brought her more publicity and notoriety, but had left her paralyzed in both legs and with a bad affliction of stuttering. But her voice and beauty were still there, and Mufson knew she would draw a big audience.

On opening night the problem of how to bring her on stage was most important, as she could not walk onto the big round twenty-four-foot stage. I came up with a bright idea. The stage moved up and down, and could disappear from stage level to twelve feet below the floor. I suggested that she get into her braced stand, which held her straight, and bring her up with the stage. They all agreed with me, and that is what we did. It worked beautifully and when I announced, "Here she is, the singing star of our show, Miss Jane Frohman," the applause was deafening. The stage came up and she started singing with her old feeling, gusto, and electrifying voice.

One of the jobs a good M.C. must learn is when to go on stage at the right time, at the end of a performer's show. Usually the performer cues the M.C. as to her last song or next to last so that he will know when to come on and bring her off. Jane Frohman never told me about her stuttering and I didn't know. Came her last song (at least I thought it was) and I came out the usual way, pointing to her and applauding her with the audience. The stage went down and up for a bow, and stopped. The audience wanted more and I foolishly went out to the center of the stage when she was standing in her braced metal standup frame and said to her aloud, "Won't you do another song for us?" She shook her head "NO, NO, NO" without saying a word and signaled for me to bring down the stage.

I did so, and finally when she came off she stuttered, "Don't you—you—ev-er—talk to me a—gain when I'm still on stage." I did not realize that once you interrupt a person who stutters, you often break their line of thought and they cannot sing or talk.

ROBERTA SHERWOOD

My first meeting with Roberta Sherwood was in Florida during the winter season of 1959 when I was entertainment director at the Eden Roc Hotel. Roberta was then featuring in a nightclub opposite the Roney Plaza owned by Murray Franklyn. He was one of the first insult comedians, long before Jack E. Leonard and Don Rickles. Walter Winchell, who stopped at the Roney Plaza, was a frequent visitor and was fascinated by this middle-aged woman who sang old nostalgic songs. He started mentioning her name in the columns and the place was packed every night as a result.

Harry Mufson, my boss at the Eden Roc, used to call on me to book the supporting acts at the Pompeii Room. If it was a comedian who was the star, we would fill in with a singer, and vice-versa. This time Joe E. Lewis was booked as the comedy star and Harry asked me to look around for a girl singer for $500 per week. I immediately thought of Roberta Sherwood and recommended her to Mufson. "What," he cried, "you want me to book that old lady, with thick glasses and a cheap fur piece around her neck, with a cymbal in her hand and hoarse voice. You must be crazy. She never played a big room like mine and would die the death of a dog."

I assured him that Roberta was very hot at the time due to the Walter Winchell plugs and that if he booked her, he would attract all the finest money people in town and get unheard of publicity. He finally agreed and I arranged an appointment with Murray Franklyn, who was a rough "dees and dose" guy who managed Roberta at that time. He aggravated Mufson with his rough talk and demands and was almost thrown out of the office. Finally, in desperation, Mufson booked her for one week at $500 for the first week, with an option to bring her back the following year at $750 per week. Well, the rest is history. Opening night, Walter Winchell introduced her and wherever Winchell went, the night crowd followed.

She was frightened as she never had sung in a large cafe the size of the Pompeii Room. I reassured her by suggesting that she walk in from the rear of the room as she had always done all her life in small nightclubs and start singing her theme song, "Love Is a Many Splendored Thing." She was a tremendous success. The boss held her over during the entire engagement of Joe E. Lewis.

We became close friends and I advised her which agent to pick among the big offers she received. She listened to my advice and chose the William Morris Office, for Sam Bramson was one of the best agents in town and I knew he would give her the best representation. As a result, in a few years her salary jumped to thousands and Mufson thanked me the next year when he brought her back at $750 per week while others paid her $5,000.

She has always shown her gratitude to me by singing a medley of Tobias songs in her act. Recently, at Jerry Van Dyke's, she included a medley of Tobias songs: "Miss You," "If I Had My Life to Live Over," and Brother Harry's "It's a Lonesome Old Town." I invited her to be our guest at the tribute to Sammy Fain given by my Hollywood Beth El Temple on March 18, 1978, at the Beverly Hilton Hotel, for which Dan Shapiro and I had been asked by Sammy to serve as co-chairmen of the entertainment committee. The following celebrities and friends of Sammy committed themselves to appear: Lt. Governor Mike Curb; Mayor Tom Bradley; George Jessel; George Burns; Mae West; Lorne Green; songwriters Paul Francis Webster, Ben Oakland, Jerry Livingston, Bernie Wayne, Richard Sherman, Jackie Barnett, Ray Evans, and Jay Livingston; Eddy Lawrence Manson; Arthur Hamilton, to present Sammy with a placque from A.S.C.A.P.; and Donald Kahn, to do likewise for A.G.A.C. At the last moment, Yip Harburg, an old friend of Sammy's, promised to be there. Roberta Sherwood was the only female entertainer on the program. As we all sang only one of Sammy's songs as a musical tribute to this wonderful guy, Roberta's only regret was that she couldn't sing the song she has used as her theme all these years, "Love Is a Many Splendored Thing."

A STAR-FILLED PLANE TRIP

It was the Christmas-New Year's holiday in 1960–1961 at the Diplomat Hotel. Every big hotel was playing a big name, and this time it was Tony Bennett at the Diplomat, Johnny Mathis at the Fountainbleau, Georgia Gibbs at the Eden Roc. Even some of the smaller hotels had fairly well known names, like Julius La Rosa, Jerry Vale, Al Martino, and others. The height of the season in Florida starts after Thanksgiving Day and drops after New Year's, then picks up again about January 15.

As usual, the greatest difficulty was getting a plane out of Miami Beach the day after New Year's, for everyone wants to leave town and it's impossible to get a reservation. I wanted to fly up north for a few weeks to visit my wife, and after getting permission, I found it difficult to book a reservation to New York. I heard that all the performers were having the same difficulty and Tony Bennett's manager decided to charter a plane for them. I heard about it and called him and asked him if I could go along in their charter plane. He graciously consented and I felt relieved that I could join them.

I think I stated before that one of the main reasons I took the jobs in Miami Beach was so that I could meet some of the big recording stars and try to get some of my songs recorded. The only one I had any luck with was Nat King Cole who had given me an hour or two while at the Eden Roc the year before. He promised to record my "Miss You" and Brother Harry's "Lonesome Old Town," and a few years later he kept his promise.

Of all the many singing stars who had recorded my songs or any Tobias songs, Tony Bennett was the only one who didn't. Suddenly I found myself on a plane with a dozen recording stars but it was a songwriter's nightmare; I didn't have a copy of any of my songs with me. Tony Bennett and the others heard about it and decided to give me the business. Each one kept coming up to me during the flight and asking if I would sing one of my songs for them. They said they would record one if they liked it. I couldn't oblige, and they laughed all the way to New York. Wow, was I embarrassed.

THE CONDOMINIUM CIRCUIT

In January of 1977 I returned from very exciting, successful, and nostalgic appearances on the condominium circuit and leading hotels in Miami Beach and Ft. Lauderdale, which I call "The Borscht Belt with Palm Trees." My last engagements in Florida were as entertainment director at the Eden Roc (1958), the Diplomat Hotel (1959), and the Fountainbleau (1961–62). At that time the Diplomat Hotel in Hollywood was the last of the large hotels built on the "Gold Strip." (The Doral was the only large hotel built after that.) There were only small hotels and empty beaches from Hollywood to Ft. Lauderdale, Florida. Now this area was full of high-rise condominiums, with prices ranging from twenty-five thousand dollars to two hundred and fifty thousand dollars each. I found a whole new audience for performers, and what an audience! All the wonderful people I met and entertained for many years in the "Borscht Belt" up north at well-known resorts such as Grossinger's, Totem Lodge, Wentworth Hall, and others, were now settled down there.

This so-called "Condo Circuit" opened up an entirely new audience for performers and a big demand for big names. Accordingly, agents like Ari Kaduri, Jerry Grant, Audrey Breen, Herb Miller and others, were booking big names such as Red Buttons, Molly Picon, Georgie Jessel, Myron Cohen, Sid Caesar, Mickey Katz, etc. I found large, modern, well-equipped theatres and auditoriums, some seating a thousand people, prevalent in such condos as Century Village, Hawaiian Village, Golden Lakes, Lauderdale West, Hallmark, Hillcrest, Jade Winds, etc., etc.

It was a pleasure and privilege to meet and greet old friends whom I had entertained in the "Borscht Belt." When I started to sing some of the old songs my brothers and I wrote through the years, like "Miss You," "Sweet and Lovely," "If I Had My Life to Live Over," "Sail Along Silvr'y Moon," "Don't Sit Under the Apple Tree," what a thrill it was to hear them sing along with me.

BOBBY BREEN

This paragraph about my trip to Florida in 1985 is added to the above, as it was then almost ten years since I last played in Florida. It was in the spring of 1985 and I had finally received a booking from an old friend, Bobby Breen, and his wife, Audre, who have become leading bookers in Florida. This time I played as a star and received star money, which was considerably more than the first time when I played with Joey Adams. Then I was accompanying him in the winter and he was the star. I finally insisted upon star billing and got it. But the story behind the bookings is more interesting in the fact that I appeared at six condos, including the leading Century City Villages in West Palm Beach, Boca Raton, and Ft. Lauderdale, where I did two a night for three nights in the hottest weather.

Bobby Breen started as a young singer in Canada at the age of twelve, almost fifty years ago. A couple of cloak-and-suit men, friends of my brother Charlie, heard him sing in Canada and were so impressed with his voice they decided to form a syndicate and finance his singing career. They knew that I was related to Eddie Cantor through marriage, so they asked me if I would bring Bobby to Eddie in California. They would pay my expenses and a few hundred dollars. I was happy to do this as I always was anxious to visit my daughter, grandchildren, and family in California during my winter months between summer work. I agreed and took Bobby out to the coast.

When Eddie Cantor heard his voice, he called me aside and said, "Henry, I hope you've got a piece of this kid."

I shyly replied, "No, I just received expenses to bring him out here and introduce him to you."

Eddie replied, "Henry, you're a schmo. This kid is going to be a big star and you could strike it rich with him." Of course it was true. He became a big star after Eddie introduced him on his program, became a star in M.G.M. movies, and the rest is history.

Fade in–Fade out.

It is now fifty years later. Bobby and his wife, Audre, are booking acts on the Condo Circuit in Florida and I have been trying to get them to book me for several years. They finally agreed and booked me during the summer months, the worst months of the year, but the salary was good and I did great. The moral of the story: Bobby Breen finally paid me off for what I did for him fifty years earlier.

I MEET THE MAFIA

I must confess that although I have been in every phase of show business since I was sixteen years old, and have worked with, was acquainted with and friendly with all kinds of people—you name them, I met them—nevertheless, I always was naive when it came to a showdown with gangsters or the Mafia. Whenever I met any notorious underground figures, I always found them very quiet, unassuming, friendly, and gentlemanly in every way.

My only experience up until 1960 with underworld figures was during a few summers as social director at Totem Lodge, which was located about twelve miles from Albany. One summer there were headlines in the papers that a well-known public figure in Albany,

Charles O'Connor, was kidnapped and that the man contacted to act as emissary for the government was an underground figure named Mushy Tractner. He used to spend the weekends at Totem Lodge and I wondered who he was and why he always had a few men with him. When he sat in the dining room, he always sat facing the door. He was a very shy and friendly man, played cards on our porch with his friends, got to know my daughter and liked her a lot. My daughter Phylis was only about ten years old at the time and I remember that one day she came to me with a ten-dollar bill in her hand. When I asked her where she got it, she replied, "Uncle Mushy gave it to me."

I asked Mushy why. He replied very affectionately, "I love that little girl and wanted to show my affection and gave her the ten dollars to buy something." I told Mushy I appreciated his thoughtfulness but I would rather she return it, and thanks anyway. It wasn't until I read the headlines in the paper that the leading Democratic figure in Albany, Charles O'Connor, had been kidnapped and Mushy was asked to be intermediator, that I knew he was in the underworld.

The next time I met any well-known underground figures was when I worked at the Diplomat Hotel in Florida during the winter of 1960, the first year it opened. I was living in a motel (now a health spa) across the street and down a few blocks on Ocean Avenue from the Diplomat. Some of the employees lived there. It was a quiet motel with about twenty-five rooms, a swimming pool in the center, and the Indian River on one side. It was owned by a man named Meyer Lansky. When I first heard that name it meant nothing to me. That's what I mean when I said, although show wise, I was naive as hell when it came to notorious names. I hadn't read any newspaper stories or books about him. All I knew was that he was a quiet little old man who walked around the pool every morning with a few men holding briefcases. I had heard from friends that he was very influential in Las Vegas.

My ambition was to land a job in Vegas someday as it was nearer to my family in California. I felt that I had had enough experience and credits as producer, director, and program director to qualify for a job there. When I heard Meyer Lansky was well known in Vegas, I approached him one day. We used to walk each day, my hand under his arm, like father and son, from the motel to the Diplomat about eleven A.M. One day I got up enough courage and confided in him. "Meyer," I said, "I've been in show business since I can remember and have produced and booked shows at large hotels and the Latin Quarter, and feel I am qualified to land an important position as entertainment director in Vegas. I heard you knew some people there and you might be able to help me."

He looked at me with a puzzled and innocent look and replied, "Where did you hear that? I don't know anyone in Vegas. Sorry, I can't be of any help to you." I took the information very disappointedly and never approached him again.

One morning we both walked to the coffee shop of the Diplomat Hotel and talked the usual small talk. He must have taken a liking to me for he asked me many times to join him for breakfast at the Diplomat Hotel. One particular morning we arrived at the coffee shop and he asked me to come over to a table in the corner and meet some of his friends. When he got to the table there were four men sitting at the back table, with their backs to the wall and looking very somber and quiet. When we approached the table they looked at me suspiciously while Meyer introduced me. "Boys, I'd like you to meet a friend of mine who works here as entertainment and program director, Henry Tobias. Henry, meet my friends: Frank Costello, Frank Ericson, and the brothers Joe and Lou Freshcetti."

I politely said, "Glad to meet you, gentlemen," and started for the door, with no intention of sitting down with them without an invitation. I started to walk out and suddenly I stopped at the door and it hit me. I did a "frozen" take. Each name was a notorious figure in the underworld. It took me some time to get over that shock after I learned who they were. I had just met four men who were actually the heads of the Mafia.

Chapter 6

The Flesh Peddlers

*C*harlie Rapp was only twelve when he observed that the super's kid, a boy soprano, went over big during the school assembly. Charley also observed that one of his father's friends, a caterer, needed entertainment on a Saturday night. Charley sold the act for ten bucks, five for the act and five for the agent. For Charley, if not for the singer, it was the beginning of a career.

A lot of jugglers, comics, baritones, novelty acts, and hoofers have gone under the bridge since then, but Charley was still selling talent as eagerly as when he was a boy.

At the age of 56 (in 1962), he had a good, solid hold on virtually every act that appeared in the Catskills during the summer madness. "I've got 175 acts signed up for 90 hotels this year," Charley said. "But it isn't all velvet. When a hotel owner has $1,500 to spend for a show, he becomes another Ziegfeld."

A short, energetic man with wispy gray hair and the mirthful mouth of a comic, Charley Rapp was the largest one-man buyer and supplier of talent around. From July 1st to Labor Day he was responsible for 98 percent of the lavish and expensive shows put on in Sullivan County.

Charley was no mere ten percenter. An adventurer, he signed his talent up at a guarantee and then proceeded to sell the act to the highest bidder. If he appraised the performer shrewdly he could, as he put it, make a buck. If a performer bombed, he took a bath.

He got his start at being more than just another agent shortly before the war when he noticed young hopefuls like Red Buttons and Jan Murray acting as social directors for $75 a week.

"I guaranteed them $150 a week and signed them up," Charley said. "I signed all the acts I could and made package deals."

Things started off smoothly but everything ground to a halt when the war broke out. Gasoline became impossible to get and he couldn't transport the talent from hotel to hotel.

"This is war—what am I going to do?" Charley would tell angry hotel owners.

"That's your problem, just deliver the acts," was the answer he would most likely receive.

Charley had no transportation problems now. Any act he signed up had to have its own car. "If a guy comes in and says I have a beautiful voice, I say, 'That's nice—what kind of a car do you have?'"

"Besides being a booking agent, I'm a transportation agent too. Suppose a comic has two shows to do in one night. When he finishes the first show, I have him pick up the prima donna and the dance team appearing down the road somewhere."

"I've got a big worksheet that tells where everyone is appearing, who has to pick up whom, how many shows are scheduled for that night—everything. Not that mistakes aren't made. . . ."

"The girl in my office once sent three top names to a bungalow colony. They played before an audience of eighty people. It had a name similar to one of the top hotels, where they should have gone."

Charley's critics say he has achieved his exalted status because some of the hotel owners are in hock to him. He admits that there is money owed to him in Sullivan County, but he sees things in another light. "Supposing you're doing business with a guy for fifteen years," he says. "You're friends by then and you love him. So he has a bad season and he puts you off. How can you press him?"

Charley Rapp, who was the leading booker of Borscht Belt acts, was reluctant to talk about the Borscht Belt. His reasons were simple. He said that if he forgot some hotel owners, he would make enemies. To play safe, he said he'd rather not mention the hotels and the owners. They were all jealous of one another. All he would say during the interview was that he started about 1938 with six hotels, including Sagamore, Laurels Country Club, Arcady, Youngs Gap House, and Totem Lodge. Now, in 1962, he was booking more than sixty hotels, almost all the best A and B class hotels.

Most of the information about his early days has been obtained from others who were associated with him, such as George Kutten, Pete Larkin, and Al Perry. Charley also had three hotels where he housed and fed his acts.

He confirmed the story about the colored act told to me by Pete Larkin. Charley's sister used to pay off the acts every week. Once Charley was sick with a high fever and a double colored act came in for payment. Charley's sister asked, "What's your name?" "Punch and Punchy." Who do you work for?" "Charley Rapp." Where did you work last week?" "No place. Every week we come in and get paid for the week, then go fishing. Never worked."

Once he sent Paul Winchell, one of his first acts, from the Laurels to Arcady Country Club—a three-hundred-mile round trip—but didn't tell him the distance. Paul traveled all night and day, did the date, and returned to the Laurels, exhausted with no sleep for two nights. He put on his swimming trunks and walked out to the pool. He had never met Charley, so he asked someone who Charley was. He was pointed out. Paul walked over and pushed Charley into the pool—and Charley couldn't even swim.

At the beginning Rapp made arrangements with one hotel president for the entertainers to eat there and he received a bill for $700 the first week. After that he paid the acts two dollars per day for food. That's when the acts could be found in front of a drugstore eating sandwiches instead of steaks.

Along about 1934 to 1938, Rapp hired three salesmen—Al Perry, Pete Larkin, and Joe Sweig—on a commission basis. They sold shows to hotel owners for every day of the week at $100 to $110 and up, took 10 percent commission. Among the early names were Red Buttons, Jan Murray, and Blackie Shackner. He hired ten or fifteen acts a week and included an eight-girl revue in the budget. He lost money in the beginning and was up to his neck in debts and trouble. That's when Kuttin joined him. Luckily he made arrangements that either party could cancel after one week.

Once Pete Larkin booked a place called Pine Tree Villa, in South

Fallsburgh. He had never been to the place and knew nothing about it but booked two solid mountain acts, Sadie Banks and Roy Gaby. Both needed music. He sent them to rehearsals and they called back to tell him that there was no music at the hotel, only a juke box. They finally scraped up a pianist.

One summer Charley took over the Empire Hotel to house and feed his acts. In one of his casual discussions with a friend of his in the due bill business, the friend asked if it would be okay to sell due bills for the Empire, since Charley wouldn't be needing all the rooms. Charley said okay, not realizing that this friend would take advantage of him. One weekend a bus rolled up and a pretty young lady stepped out, informed the man in charge, Joe Sweiger, that she had a due bill reservation for this hotel and asked about the entertainment. In order to please this one person, all the acts put on a show after finishing their various chores at the hotels. She got an all-star show featuring Jan Murray, Red Buttons, and all the other acts that worked for Charley. She sat out front all alone, attired in an evening gown and enjoying it immensely.

Buddy Hackett and many other acts used to do six shows for $90 plus an extra $10 for the use of the car. Sometimes they were lucky and had to travel only a few miles between engagements, but sometimes Rapp and Larkin would send them more than 100 miles to places such as Copake. The big problem during the war was gas rationing. A common practice was to push the speedometer back so they could get gas from ration tickets (determined by mileage). They drove the gas station man crazy coming back so often with the same car and a different story.

Charley Rapp could afford to finance several of the hotels he provided with entertainment and thus became the owner's good friend. If an owner ran into a bad week or two because of a rainy spell and held back Rapp's checks, Rapp carried them. Having many accounts and doing a large gross business, Rapp could afford to extend credit. Sometimes this ran into thousands of dollars and sometimes he lost out because of bankruptcies. However, he never lost the good will of the owner, who became more obligated to him. Charley became the biggest booker in the Borscht Belt, at one time booking more than 70 hotels involving hundreds of acts, doing a gross business of a million a year, leaving him a handsome profit of a hundred thousand or so. He could afford the gamble and lose ten or twenty thousand with bankrupt honest, or sometimes unethical, owners.

As an example and proof of this, my ruthless and unethical boss, David M. Katz, as we explained in another chapter, took advantage of the situation where Charlie Rapp was concerned.

It was in the summer of 1957 when Totem Lodge was about to go bankrupt. I saw the handwriting on the wall and that the big bubble was about to burst. In a few years Katz had let the indebtedness grow from $50,000 to $500,000. I could feel the uneasiness and continued restlessness of his creditors and knew he was ready for another bankruptcy.

Charley Rapp was furnishing the entertainment on a budget averaging $500 per week and Katz had built up his indebtedness to Charley to about $10,000 near the end of the summer. I had continually warned Charley not to give him any more credit, for I knew what was going to happen. Despite my loyalty to Katz as an employer, I was also a performer at heart and felt responsible for Rapp getting into this mess. I knew that after Totem went I would still need Rapp's friendship and have to do business with him.

Rapp heeded my advice, but a little too late. In late August he insisted on being paid cash before the acts went on. Katz acted insulted and blamed me for the situation. I was in a spot. I had to be loyal to Totem and deliver to my guests for the sake of my reputation, and so I personally guaranteed (with a signed note) to cover the payments of the last shows. The amount was only $1,000, and Katz owed Rapp much more—about $10,000. You guessed it. He paid Rapp with postdated checks that bounced. Rapp, being an old friend of mine and used to these kinds of dealings and knowing that I could not afford the $1,000 guarantee, generously tore up my notes. He never collected from Katz and still brings up the fact that I got him into that hole. I have since found out that Totem was not the only one of Rapp's financial losses. His generosity as far as I'm concerned was most appreciated and whenever I can, I show this appreciation. I did it in a most practical manner. At the end of the summer of 1958 (last year at Totem), I took a trip with Rapp to the White Mountains ("Blue Borscht Belt") where I personally introduced him to the owners of the Maplewood, Sinclair, Wentworth Hall, and Mt. Washington hotels and succeeded in getting him those accounts.

I first met Charley Rapp at Totem about 1942 when I returned as social director. He had visited us as a guest before and had always tried to book our entertainment.

The Morris Agency would no longer handle low-budget accounts of $10,000 per year or less. I convinced Katz that Rapp was the logical man to book our shows. He could obtain "NAMES" at lower cost than the Morris Agency, for he was in a position to guarantee these names a series of bookings, representing several hotels, and in this way keep within our budget.

Charlie has been accused of buying acts sight unseen, like breakfast cereal in a supermarket. "That's not completely true," Charlie said. "I read *Variety* and have a retentive memory. When an act comes in looking for work, I know where they worked last, what their notices are like, and how they'll fit in with the type package I'm setting up. And if I don't know about them, I can make a couple of phone calls and find out all I need to know. When an act walks in, after one or two questions, I can tell what they're worth."

Not that Charley claims to be infallible. Some years back he hired a young singer for $35 for a night's work. The singer tried to get a raise to $50 and Charley fired him. The fellow's name is Eddie Fisher.

One of Charley's problems was seeing that the act fit the place. "In some places they don't want Myron Cohen," he said, "because that's the way the customers talk normally."

The first time I sent "Fat Jack" Leonard to the mountains, I sent him to a place where they had a lot of guys with yamulkahs sitting around. His opening line was, "Welcome Legionnaires."

"When an act bombs, I'm the one the hotel owners blame; even if they insisted on that act, they still blame me. 'Why did you let me do it?' they'll ask."

Entertainers, of course, are another problem. "Entertainers are like children," he says. "You've got to know how to handle them. I used to hurt them but I stopped that. I see them crying and figured I shouldn't be so rough. Now I try to let them down as easily as possible."

In Charley's world the most valued entertainers are the comics. One comic is worth 500 baritones. "One time I had this bulvan (Yiddish for "strong boy") working for me. We had Lenny Kent signed up to do one show on a Saturday for $200. On Saturday Kent walks into the office and says he got an offer to do two shows for $200 each. Unless we get him another show to do, the deal's off. The bulvan went crazy and grabbed the comic by the neck. I managed to pull him off and Lenny ran away. After it was over I told him, 'Listen, if you want to hit a baritone or prima donna, go ahead.

But as long as you work for me, never hit a comic. They're too hard to get.'"

I read a magazine article written in 1965 about Charlie Rapp, that stated the following:

" A mere 90 minutes from Broadway, vaudeville is still very much alive and kicking. Here in the Catskill Mountains abound more than 300 hotels that provide a mecca of entertainment for more than 2,000,000 customers each year."

The stages of these hotels use nearly 1,000 performers, with acts ranging from dance teams and variety acts to singers and comedians. The quality runs the gamut from an unknown at $35 a show to a Barbra Streisand or Sammy Davis, Jr., at better than $5,000. The "Borscht Circuit" offers unparalleled facilities, from food to fun-in-the-sun by day, but at night the exhausted vacationers expect to sit back and be entertained—with a different show every night.

Small hotels feature only a few shows a week; the larger ones put on as many as eight. There are shows at some hotels year round, but the peak demand for talent comes during the ten-week period ending on Labor Day. The overwhelming task of filling the stages falls on the shoulders of a small group of men called "bookers," and the kingpin of them all is 60-year-old Charles Rapp.

The stocky, balding president of National Television and Radio Artists books most of the talent used by 75 percent of the larger hotels—Grossinger's and the Concord, two exceptions, book their own. Rapp is referred to as the "King of the Mountains," and he is rarely found with less than a telephone in each hand. His office at 1650 Broadway looks like a bookie parlor, with people sitting at battered desks and a battery of telephones going.

The walls are filled with names and numbers of agents, hotels, big stars, and many Catskill perennials whose acts have been on the Borscht Circuit for years but are virtually unknown elsewhere.

A quarter of a century ago, when Charley Rapp started booking acts, he found it necessary to be "not only a booker, but a nursemaid, travel agent, and missing persons bureau. My biggest problem then was not placing the talent, but seeing to it that they got there—on time—and had a place to spend the night. They had to be rested and fresh for the next show in another hotel the following night.

"Today, the Thruway has alleviated the problem of acts getting lost on a small, out-of-the-way dirt road, but they still have to sleep."

To accommodate the performers, Charley acquired two hotels of his own, the Willow Lane in Monticello and the Midwood in Hurleyville. These are used strictly to house the acts between shows.

"Anybody who thinks he has talent eventually comes knocking on our door," Rapp says. If an act has no credits, he might set up a midnight club date, and either he or his nephew Joey will take a look at them. "I can remember," says Charley, "when one of my associates told me that Lew Mason, the comic, was just seen drinking a malted in Hanson's Drug Store downstairs. As he was telling me, a hotel called with a plea for a comedian for that very night.

"I ran downstairs and he said he was a comedian and it was about time we noticed him. He turned out to be Jackie and not Lew, but I took a chance and booked him for 25 bucks. Today I pay Jackie Mason a hundred times that much for a single performance."

Years ago, when the hotels had Jerry Lewis working as a busboy, and Eddie Fisher, Danny Kaye, and Buddy Hackett were working at jobs ranging from bellhops to social directors, Charley had an idea. He bought a hotel, stocked it with performers whom he paid a flat salary, and then went out and booked them into the other hotels at a profit.

The acts were pleased because they were getting paid and didn't have to carry bags or dishes. The hotel became known as "Rapp's Paradise," and Charley had nearly a hundred assorted performers on tap. "It was quite an investment," he recalls, "but it paid off."

To utilize the unoccupied rooms, Rapp began to rent to anybody who wanted them. One day two young secretaries checked in and later that night, true to Catskill tradition, wanted to be entertained. "Well, it was a show that will go down in the annals of show business," Charley beams. "Those two girls, the whole audience, were entertained by 80 acts who had no other shows that night. And the headliners were Red Buttons and Robert Merrill!"

Charley Rapp had much to do with the beginning of many stars. In 1945, for example, ex-GI Buddy Hackett approached him for some work. Charley offered him the job of social director of Grossinger's.

"I asked for $75 a week," Buddy recalls, "and Charley said $30. Close enough, I said—and took it."

From there, Buddy made the rounds, earning up to $15 a performance. Later the star of Broadway's "I Had a Ball" worked only the Concord, except for an occasional show at the Tamarack in Ellinville, where he works free.

"The owner, Dave Levinson," Buddy explains, "found work for my father and me when we needed it read bad. My Dad was an upholsterer, working the resort hotels, fixing their furniture. I used to help him when I was about fourteen, and Dave was a real person. I don't forget things like that."

Booking acts for hotels is not only lucrative, it is a way of life, consuming as many as eighteen hours a day. Rapp has to be ready to fill a spot at a moment's notice. An act gets sick, or the owner of a small hotel expects 200 people for the weekend and, at the last minute, 400 arrive. The hotel man, who may originally have requested only a comedian, now wants a complete show. Charley will sign some performers at a flat rate for the ten-week season, which is why a hotel that can't afford more than, say, $350 for a whole show, might get a comic worth that much—plus a singer and a dance team.

The Borscht Circuit is legendary as the training ground of talent. The acts, though, have to prove themselves, and they work very hard at it. The public is a difficult taskmaster and the great aim is to get the vacationers to remember your name. If they do, the word goes out and once in a while a star is born.

The comedy act of Chase and Reed reminds one of the old Martin-Lewis act. Dick Chase started singing in the mountains when he was twenty-two years old, but his cutting up caused him to switch to comedy and team up with Morton Reed. Their antics led to very steady work, good money, and a hectic pace that would stun a Madison Avenue account executive. Take a typical week:

Sunday night—a 10:30 show at the Granit, sleep at the hotel. Monday—time for a swim (maybe), drive to the Laurels, rehearse for a couple of hours. Show time, 10:30 to 1 A.M. Sleep. Tuesday—brunch, time for a sunbath (maybe), drive to the Nevele. Another rehearsal (different lights, different band, different stage). Showtime, 10:30. Repeat for Wednesday (The Pines), Thursday (Brown's), Friday (Tamarack). Saturday, the real pressure begins with an early show at a bungalow colony at 9:00 P.M., a quick drive to the Gradus for the 11 o'clock show, another night drive to reach the Concord just in time for the late show at 1:30 A.M.

No wonder they sleep late on Sundays! All the Borscht Belt entertainers are certain they will hit the very big time. They complain about the hard hours, the treadmill of work, the pay that they feel is never commensurate with their talent, and the rat race. But one comic, who earns better than $40,000 a year, owns a beautiful home and a new Cadillac and is debt-free, tells us, "Where else can I earn such money? After all these years, I know that I'm conning myself when I believe that I'm going to hit it big. But if I lose that feeling, I'm finished. Because without that, I'd hate it!"

Singers are not as difficult to obtain as comics, so the law of supply and demand takes over. They are also not as angry, nor are most of them as well known, but they have their own problems. Lovely Brooklyn-born Sally Russell, who has been supporting her four children since her husband died, invested $6,000 in her current act. She pays an arranger $200 for every song in her repertoire. The payoff—$75 a show.

Why does she do it? "Because I love to be in front of an audience, and because this is only the beginning. Maybe Johnny or Ed Sullivan will see me—and then you'll be able to multiply that $75 by ten."

Black singer Mauri Leighton not only loves applause, she loves the mountains and the people. And beautiful Laura Lane agrees—"I make a good living from those beautiful Catskills."

It's been a long road from bingo in the lobby and gin rummy in the dining room to the elaborate casinos and nightclubs of today's Catskill resorts. The big change took place in 1955, when the Concord Hotel opened the first nightclub in the Catskills. It is the largest nightclub in the world, seating over 3,000.

The Winarick family, owners of the Jeris Hair Tonic Company, built the Concord on beautiful Kiamesha Lake, in scenic Sullivan County. In 1935 they hired 17-year-old Phil Greenwald as a lifeguard. Phil was soon promoted to athletic director, and also found himself working for Jeris as a salesman.

Then, sensing a trend in the trickle of big-name entertainers who were even then pulling customers to the Catskills, the late Arthur Winarick decided to use name talent to lure more business to his hotel. The job of booking the names fell on young Phil. This was the turning point on the Borscht Circuit. The rivalry between Grossinger's and the Concord splashed over to other hotels and the battle was on.

But the boom took time to gather steam. At first, Phil's pleas to various performers fell on deaf ears. Money meant nothing to the stars, who would not gamble their reputations in the mountains, not even for a single show.

Phil turned to an old friend, Tony Martin. He pleaded with the handsome singer, and Tony gave in. "I then went to another pal, Milton Berle. He didn't say no, either. I owe them everything," Phil says.

Thus the tide changed and things got easier. Others saw what had happened, and followed Martin's and Berle's lead. Today the Concord offers almost every top name in show biz. Most command much more than Phil can pay them, but everybody seems to belong to the "I Love Philly Greenwald Club."

One of Charley's biggest problems was finding the right type of act for the particular type of crowd the hotel was going to have on any certain date. "If we're having an insurance company convention, I can't have the same type of act that would appeal to a B'nai B'rith lodge."

Gambling crowds still flock to Las Vegas or Puerto Rico, and the warm weather seekers fly to Miami, but thanks to the Charley Rapps and the Philly Greenwalds, Broadway heads for the mountains.

HENRY STERN

In my constant search for more information about the old days in the Borscht Belt, I received the following information in January 1965 from Henry Stern, one of the most active Borscht Belt agents in those days. He showed me contracts from his files:

Gene Barry was first hired by the Congress Hotel in Sackett Lake, New York, for a salary of $16.50 per week.

Sid Caesar, who was then named Sidney Caesar, was first hired as sax and clarinet player with a five-piece band at Vacationland Hotel in 1939. The salary for the entire orchestra was $60 per week. In 1941 he started as staff comedian at Kutchers Country Club and received for his services, from July to Labor Day, the total sum of $100.

Red Buttons. In 1940, Red received a contract from Kenmore Lake Hotel, located in Livingston Manor, for $50 per week.

Joe E. Ross worked as top comic at the Windsor Hotel in South Fallsburgh for $50 per week.

Eli Basse started as comedian and received $75 a week at the Lakeside Inn.

DAVE STERN

The latest interview about the Borscht Belt took place at my home here in Hollywood on December 2, 1978, with Dave Stern, who was one of the top bookers in the old days during the beginning of the Borscht Belt era. He told me the true story about Jerry Lewis's start in show business, in which he played an important part.

I wrote about my refusing Jerry $5 to appear in one of my amateur shows at Totem—that was the year of 1942, when Jerry was 16 years old and working in a drug store at Averill Park near Totem. Now Dave Stern takes the story from there.

During the summer of 1943, Danny Lewis, Jerry's father, worked at Brown's Hotel as M.C. His wife played the piano and his son, Jerry, then only 17 years old, worked in the kitchen as a busboy. Once a week during the big show, Danny would introduce his son who did a pantomime act with a record machine in which he acted out the voice of the recording artist while the record played over the public address system. At the end of the summer Danny came to Dave Stern's office and told him how great his son was and pleaded for Dave to give him a job in one of his theatres.

Dave explained to Danny that he booked more than one hundred theatres run by Warners, R.K.O., and Skouras, and played only known, established acts. Danny was persistent and kept bothering Dave until he decided to take a chance for free, and put Jerry on at one of his theatres in New Jersey. He played eight acts and had to cut each act down a few minutes in order to give Jerry seven or eight minutes.

He opened the show with Jerry, who stopped the audience cold. The manager ran back and they decided to put him on third during the second show. He was so strong and great they put him on next to closing in the third supper show. Nobody could follow him so they closed with him on the fourth and last show. It was the Orpheum Theatre in Newark, New Jersey, and they kept him over for three days. He was as skinny as the microphone but full of talent and energy.

Danny was very excited about his first break and pleaded with Dave to handle him. Dave told him he was a booker, not a manager, but recommended Abner Greshler. Abby booked him into the Havana Madrid where the star of the show was singer Dean Martin. Dean was getting $110 a week and Jerry, $85. After the third night Abner Greshler came to see them again and they were getting big laughs doing an afterpiece together after the show. Abby told them to keep it in and signed with them as manager. He booked them into the 500 Club in Atlantic City and from there on the rest is history. Later, when Dave Stern wanted to book them for a single night's engagement at the Waldorf Astoria, they held him up for $750 and he had to pay it.

Time did not permit us to talk more than one half hour and in this time Dave Stern told me that the following acts played for him sometime during their early beginnings at one or all of the hundred or more theatres he booked in New York, independent theatres owned by Rosenthal and Blatt:

Burt Lancaster, who started as bottom man in an acrobatic act during the early '40s; Robert Alda, Jack Albertson, Joey Faye, Liberace, Milton Berle, when he first worked with a girl partner by the name of Kennedy. The act was called Kennedy and Berle . . . Red Buttons, Buddy Ebson and sister Wilma. Gus Van after his partner Schenck died. Pat Rooney and his son Junior. Dave tells me that old man Pat stole his son's girl from him and married her. Baby Rose Marie, Buddy Howe, Larry Storch, Larry Best, Carl Reiner, Jack Carter and Ross Martin plus Dick Shawn, who was handled by Bobby Bernard at that time, and Freddy Prinz, and his manager Dave Jonas.

The Dave Jonas/Freddy Prinz association deserves a paragraph. It was a known fact that many small agents and managers found some of the big names of today and nursed them and worked with them, until they finally reached the point where their talents were recognized. At that time usually the big agencies, such as William Morris, MCA, ABC, and the likes would step in, sometimes to buy their contracts from the small agent or most of the time just to steal them away by luring the act with a big bonus. Such was the case with Dick Shawn and Bobby Bernard, who finally was forced to sell Dick to a big agency for little money.

In the case of Dave Jonas, he found Freddy Prinz when he was still in his teens, signed him to a strong legal contract with signatures by his parents. After Freddy switched to a big agency without paying Jonas anything, and then became a big TV star, Jonas spent five years in court suing Freddy. Finally the sad ending, but not so sad for Jonas. After Freddy committed suicide, Jonas finally won the case and was awarded over $200,000, which left the Prinz family destitute, but for which Dave Jonas received his just reward.

Al Rock

"I started in show business as one-half of a two-man comedy act called Stanton & Rock (Stanton was Jack Soble), singing and talking. The year was about 1931. One of the Evans boys, owners of Evans Hotel in Lock Sheldrake, caught my act at a Fally Marcus Theatre in Brooklyn and offered me the job as social director. It was the first time they ever had a social director. The old man Evans couldn't understand why a fellow who sings songs should also be paid. It was enough that he was a Free Eater (Ooomzistiker Fresser).

"There was no one else on the staff, just me and the band. I had to do everything, just as many other social directors in that day, had to dream up different entertainment for every day in the week and get talent wherever I could find it, from guests, staff, help, etc. The old man Evans practically owned the entire town of Lock Sheldrake. He was a deputy sheriff and landlord of most of the stores in town. This is how many hotel owners started building hotels. They had it coming from all sides. I worked at Evans for three years in a row, five-piece band, no bookers.

"After that I went to Swan Lake Inn, in Swan Lake, N.Y., and on my staff was Henny Youngman, who was only my comedy stooge. He had left his violin playing behind. He received no salary at all, but was paid off by selling raffles all summer long and running a few affairs for the staff—him and me, that's how he made his expenses. The owners were two high school principals and the farmer who owned the hotel. From there I went to Shawanga Lodge, in 1936, and finished my career as a Catskill Mountain M.C. (social director) after that engagement. I entered the booking business and refused to book any hotels for I thought this was the worst part of show business, knowing the owners as I did. I did visit these hotels often and entertained for free board.

"Abbey Greshler was recommended to me in 1938, and I took him into my office where he booked small bands and social directors for resorts. The first big accounts he brought in were the Grand Hotel in High Mount, which was the first hotel to play big names; Griswald Hotel in New London, Ct.; Hollywood Hotel in West End; and Laurel in the Pines in Lakewood. All the biggest names were brought in for free to most of these hotels; that's how Abbey got his reputation and got to book many hotels.

"Some of the big names booked at that time were Willie Howard, Georgie Price, Ethel Merman, Cab Callaway, Jan Murray, Ritz Brothers, Jan Bart, Michele Rosenberg, Moyshe Oyshe, and the Barry Sisters (then known as Bagelman Sisters).

"Some of the early social directors were Jimmy Buster, Mike Hammer, Lou Brown, Mopey & Dopey (George Gardner and Al Green), Lou Saxon (who was then known as Shatz), Julie Oshins, Joey Abrams, etc., etc. Abbey Greshler was with me for three years, then left to go on his own."

VIC MIZZY

Well-known songwriter Vic Mizzy, writer of such hits as "My Dreams Are Getting Better All the Time," "Take It Easy," "The James Boys," and composer of the TV shows "Adams Family" and "Kentucky Jones" fills in some of the facts about Abner Greshler. When Vic was 14 years old he was hired as a substitute pianist at the Hotel Regal in Fallsburgh, N.Y., with the Danny Stroller Orchestra, consisting of seven men with a salary of $7.50 a week. Abbey booked the band and got 75¢ commission from each man. He was so young that he had to paint a moustache on his lip so that he would look older, as the owners complained about "those kids." The social director was an Italian, Charlie Samuels, who used that name so he could work in a Jewish place. Henry Nemo was comedian. He says Abbey was the king of the agents before Beckman & Pransky.

When it got busy at Green's Hotel, the bosses would move the band out of the social hall where they slept and move the guests into their rooms. That's when the band would sleep on the lawn. Abner Greshler's mother found him sleeping on the lawn.

Abbey would move the furniture from the lobby into the social hall to be used for the show, and the bosses would scream when the lobby was empty and all the furniture missing. Also, they would cut down trees and bushes and flowers to use on the stage and leave the hotel grounds bare and the boss screaming.

Abner Greshler was the first agent who could speak with five syllable words. He was educated and passed the bar examination. When he told people he was going to Fordham University, they thought he was a gentile.

The bosses wanted to fire Vic Mizzy because he was always playing practical jokes on everyone. The band once lived in three rooms marked "DO NOT DISTURB" that belonged to the guests. No one ever caught on. Mike Hammer was called "Sniffy" because he sniffed all the time.

Abbey relates that one of his most effective weapons to grab hotel accounts away from his competitors was to give them free entertainment. Another method was to get vaudeville headliners who were in between engagements and invite them for a week or two vacation as guests, with the promise that he would try and get some dates for them. In this way he was able to offer more free big-time entertainment than anyone else.

When the boss of one place asked him, "How about a bonfire?" Abbey had never heard of it, and made a fire in the middle of the brand new tennis court, ruining a $2,000 project, and almost causing a fire that would have destroyed the whole hotel.

ABNER J. GRESHLER

One of the important pioneer agents in the Borscht Belt, together with Beckman and Pransky, George Kuttin, Mike Hammer, and others, was Abner Greshler, now one of the most important and influential agents and personal representatives in Hollywood, who handles such top names as Tony Randall, Vincent Edwards, Mort Sahl, Don Knotts, Frank Tashlin, and many others, and was responsible for discovering and putting together Martin and Lewis. He also gave Buddy Hackett his stage name.

Greshler recalls his early beginning when he was just out of high school and going to Fordham University to study law. He was helping his uncle in the fur business deliver packages. Even in those days he would let the others do the heavy work and collect the profit. He hired boys to deliver and went along to make sure they collected. He met the Kaminsky brothers who owned a hotel called Esther Manor in Greenfield Park, New York. This is how he started in the Borscht Belt. He used to do a tap dance when he delivered the fur pieces for his uncle. The Kaminsky brothers were in the clothing business too and one of them said to Abbey, "You would make a good meshuginer."

Abbey answered, "What do you mean?"

"I mean a social DRECK. He told his Mom and Dad he wanted to become a social director in the mountains. He was only seventeen years old, but grew a moustache so he would look older. He weighed 200 pounds in those days. They objected, said he would become a bum.

His cousin Panzer had a hotel called Wellworth Hotel in Hurleyville. She advised his parents not to let him take the job, that he would become a bum. He accepted the job.

Even in those days, though broke and only seventeen, he hired a chauffeur and rented an Iosha Francini, foreign car, from Harold Stern, the orchestra leader who later became his client.

At the Palace Cafeteria on 46th Street, he met all the boys, bought the usual necessary material of skits and jokes from the usual characters, Joey Faye, etc. This is the place where one act would sneak the check out to his friend so his friend could come in and finish his meal. Jack Diamond was another fellow who sold material together with Charlie, a well-known material seller.

It was at his first job at Esther Manor that he learned of two affairs for the staff. He didn't know what they meant when they said "affairs." The boys in the cafeteria explained it to him. So they printed up tickets for the affair. The first affair was a "Kiddie Night." There were four hundred guests and Abbey sold 385 tickets for one dollar each. When the boss, Kaminsky, wanted one half, he refused. He gave the band $50 and kept the rest.

It was then he first learned about agents. George Kuttin was agent for the band and the orchestra leader told him he had to pay him 10 percent of his earnings. That's when he decided to become an agent. He had Hank Henry, Jack Diamond, and Janis Williams the dancer on his staff. Janis used to teach the kids dancing for $1. Abbey would split it with her.

He hired a fellow by the name of Bernie Edison, who had a car. He was not yet seventeen years old. They went around and booked several places in Fallsburgh. He arranged for acts out of work to spend a week at a hotel, with the promise to look for work. For the free room and board the act would entertain. This free entertainment is what helped Abbey get more hotel accounts. Pretty soon he was the "King."

While at Esther Manor he exchanged entertainment with Tamarack Lodge. This was known as Guest Night. One staff would entertain at the other spot one night a week, and vice-versa, giving each hotel a free show.

Abbey played the amateur circuit like many of us did for Irving Barrett and his brother Marty Barrett, doing recitations of serious poems like "My Little Rosa" (Italian dramatic bit).

He booked Paul Tremaine and his orchestra as the first big-time band.

His first big account was The High Mount, in High Mount, N.Y., once owned by the railroad company and now by Frank Seiden. It was here, about 1935–1937, that Abbey started bringing up high class entertainment. He knew Rudolph Bing of the Metropolitan and booked such artists as Sid Lewis, Nannette Gilford, and others.

He says Jan Peerce started as a violinist with Jack Berger's Band.

It was at the Flagler about 1938 that he worked with Dore Schary. This was the first regular theatre with seats and first stage ever to be able to fly scenery in the Catskills. They also were the first hotel that had a nine-hole golf course, about 1936.

Some of the big names he played for Seiden for free were Ethel Merman, Georgie Jessel, Georgie Price, and The Hartmans. He covered the pit orchestra to give the stage more room. Sam Leve was their art director.

At Swan Lake the owners interviewed social directors. The owner asked one social director, "What do you plan to do on Mondays?

S.D.:   On Mondays it's Game Night.
OWNER: What do you intend to do on Tuesday?
S.D.:   Tuesdays is Semifinals.
OWNER: What Semifinals?
S.D.:   Semifinals of the Monday night games.
OWNER: And Wednesday?
S.D.:   To tell you the truth, the guests will be so tired from Monday and Tuesday that they wouldn't want anything on Wednesday. Thursday is Proscenium Night.
OWNER: What's that?

S.D.:   The M.C. comes out and announces that the curtain over
          the stage is a proscenium and it works up and down. After
          spending some time explaining and showing what a pros-
          cenium is, they announce the big show for Friday and
          Saturday.

Whitey Trager whose father was vice-president of Bank of United
States, was the band leader of an 18-piece orchestra. Each got $12 a
week, less 10 percent commission.

Abbey booked Camp Tamiment entertainment and claims he
helped book Max Liebman. He booked shows before Liebman, took
the Straw Hat Revue out of Tamiment, and sold it to Shuberts.

Abbey says they started a "Social Directors Association" and has a
program to prove it. Some members were Harry Cutler, Lou Saxon,
Buddy Walker, Larry Best, Buddy Hackett, Van Johnson, Julie Oshins, Sonny Tufts.

The old agents who started the Resort Entertainment Bureau
with him were Mike Hammer, Beckman and Pransky, George Kuttin, Phil Gross, Harold Kahn, and Al Lyons. This was about 1936–
1937. They booked the William B. Friedland units. Jerry Lewis
worked with his Dad and Mom at Green's. Jerry was only twelve and
"toomeled up" plenty then.

Abbey's story about the gangsters follows. He admits that Beck-
man got into trouble with the mob but he kept it to himself, and
Abbey who worked with them and Pransky knew nothing about it.
In order to get the hood off, Beckman told one of the mob to see
Abbey Greshler and that he would take care of him.

One day a notorious mobster, Chink Sherman, walked up to
Abbey and demanded a cut. Abbey was flabbergasted and knew
what it meant to refuse. He asked for some time to talk it over with
his associates, Beckman and Pransky. He then went to his personal
buddy, Erickman, who was one of the top brass among the country's
mobsters. He told him the story and never heard from Chink Sherman again. He feels that this is what took Beckman off the spot.

MARTY BAUM

Marty Baum was vice president of Ashley-Famous Artists Agency.
He and Abe Newborn worked for Jules Zeigler as ex-G.I.s and
decided to enter the agency business in 1950 representing two

broken down acts, The Duffys and Catron Brothers. They placed an ad in a trade paper stating that they were starting in business. Jack Golbert who was Entertainment and Program Director at Lake Tarleton in Pike, N.H., owned by Walter Jacobs, had an idea that he could organize a circuit in that area (called the Blue Borscht Circuit), consisting of Sagamore Hotel in Lake George, N.Y. (owned by Lou Brandt); Lake Tarleton, Pike, N.Y. (Walter Jacobs); The Maplewood, Bethlehem, N.Y.; The Sinclair Hotel and Parkview in Bethlehem, N.Y.; Mt. Washington Hotel, Bretton Woods, N.Y.; Lake Spafford Hotel, Lake Spafford, N.Y. (Abe Jacobson, owner); Wentworth Hall, Jackson, N.Y. (owned by Harry Scheiner); Greys Inn, Jackson, N.Y. (then owned by E. M. Loew).

He read Baum & Newborn's ad and was looking for unknown new agents to make a deal with. He walked into their office and asked them if they would be interested in booking eight hotels. You can imagine their reaction. They were earning $25 a week as ex-G.I.'s pension. They grabbed the deal and made arrangements to book acts at regular 10% commission from the acts, no weekly deal with guarantee, just regular actor's commission. Jack Goldbert organized the owners and got them all to agree, at similar budget, with a small one for doubling to two hotels on one night in Bethlehem and a double between Mt. Washington and one hotel, Parkview, in Bethlehem (20 miles distant).

The hotels wanted more sophisticated entertainment than the usual run of the mill Borscht Belt acts, so they booked some of the following performers: Harry Belafonte ($75 a night); Alan King ($100 a night); Zero Mostel ($50); and Lenny Bruce (who did a clean act those days, $50). They never saw or visited the hotels until the last week of the season when they drove up in a new car (Marty on his honeymoon almost got killed on a winding road near Tarleton. The car was demolished, but Abe Newborn was reading a paper when it happened and yelled to his partner, "Hey Marty, quit kidding around.")

NATHAN A. ABRAMSON

Another offshoot of the Borscht Belt is the "High Seas Circuit," developed and started by Nat Abramson, now deceased, and continued by his son Ephraem Abramson, head of W.O.R. Artists Bureau.

Nat Abramson was born in the Borscht Belt. His parents owned the Central House in Hunter, N.Y. Nat started producing, directing, and social directing at an early age, at first just to please his parents' guests, and later developed into one of the leading bookers in the entertainment field.

From this humble beginning in Hunter he developed a taste for the finer arts and started booking classical singers, dancers and musicians for club dates, mostly long hair talent. He ran the first commerical cruise for the Level Club, an organization of wealthy men in the mid-Manhattan area, who chartered the "Mauretania," a Cunard liner. He was the first impressario who produced large shows on ships, and from this he became the largest booker of entertainment on the high seas. He handled as many as fifty ships at one time and presented every kind of entertainment, including well-known names.

He organized and started the first Resort Managers Association as early as 1930 and became its president and spokesman. He concentrated mostly on club jobs, concerts, industrial shows, and ships; but booking entertainment for ships became the office's specialty.

His son Ephraem explains that each ship has its own personality, and certain cruises and lines such as Holland American, which attract very high-class Jewish American clientele like the Grossinger and Concord crowd, must be entertained accordingly. So on these trips he books the regular Borscht Belt entertainment program. On other ships, like the Canadian American, he books more classical and conservative entertainment. Some ships attract the country-club crowd and so each ship must have certain entertainers according to its clientele. The ships have taken a great part of the Borscht Belt business away, for people have become travel conscious and get tired of going to the mountains. He feels that in order to meet the stiff competition he must give twice as much and better entertainment than the Borscht Belt.

Nat Abramson owned a home in Hunter called "10 percent Acres."

SHOW BUDGETS

To give you an example of budgets in the industry, I kept the budget at Totem Lodge down to less than $12,000 for the entire summer. This included my salary, that of the band, and a girl singer. The dance team usually paid the hotel for the concession, so they drew no salary. Included in the above amount was the cost of renting ten movie films, shown weekly, and the projectionist's fee of $25 per showing. The film rentals ran about $50 to $100 per showing.

In 1939, when I left to go to Grossinger's, Katz decided to go in for "names"; naturally he had to seek a big name agency, William Morris Agency, for the attractions he wanted. They and MCA controlled most of the big stars. Some of those who appeared during the summers of 1939 to 1941 were: Milton Berle, Joe E. Lewis, Sophie Tucker, Harry Richman, the Andrews Sisters, Joey Adams, Henny Youngman, Myron Cohen, Jackie Miles, and Sam Levinson, and others who were popular then.

For the time that this policy was in effect, Totem Lodge spent $25,000 or more during those summers, each season—more than twice what I spent without names. But we offered entertainment all week long. The "names" were only of value publicity-wise for newspapers and word of mouth. They brought in no additional revenue except perhaps a few dollars on Saturday night when Katz would charge the local citizens (from Troy, Albany, Schnectady and other nearby villages) $5 for supper and show.

It just wasn't in the cards to continue on such a large budget, and when the United States got into the war in 1942, he rehired me at a big reduction in salary. He dropped his entertainment budget to about $10,000. I don't know what the budgets were at similar summer adult camps like Totem, such as Scaroon Manor, Tamiment, Green Mansions, Copake, or Berkshire Country Club.

Chapter 7

More Borscht Belt Alumni Stories

*T*he first "toomler" back in the early days of the boarding house was born out of necessity. When the hotel owner started to grow, so did his guests' complaints, and in order to escape these complaints, he looked for a scapegoat. It was usually the "life of the party" on his staff, sometimes a musician, sometimes a waiter, busboy, or bellhop—whoever looked as if he could entertain the guests for free was usually the one the boss selected as his "life of the party," "social director," "toomler." He would pay him a few dollars extra a week, or give him some extra privileges to do the extra work.

Sometimes the staff would give the boss extra privileges in order to have the experience of entertaining and learning. For instance, Sid Caesar played the sax in the band for the first few years but he

93

was doing comedy on the side, and in order to leave his musician work and enter the field, he took a cut of five dollars a week.

So the boss had a scapegoat and every time a guest complained about anything, he would see the social director, so all complaints were placed with him. When a guest left his wife and children for the week, he came to the social director. "Don't forget, take care of my wife." Little did he know, the social director took him literally. Even when the guest complained about the food or the rooms or the toilets or the leaks or the lights, "See the Social." The "social" had to arrange card games and tournaments so that the Carlottas could meet the boys, take hikes, enter swimming events, and everything. He was the shad chan, babysitter, pimp, whoremaster, card shark, lecturer, sing-along with Hymie; and if he had a few hours off, he would have to shop around for some of the items the guests needed. Whenever he went to town they grabbed him and gave him a list of things to buy and do. More and more the owner passed the buck to him, and soon he needed assistance. That's how the staff was born.

ALAN TRESSER

On April 23, 1966, when I walked into the Fallsview Hotel in Ellenville, I felt as if I were back at Totem Lodge in the early days. I couldn't believe my eyes. There was a guy who looked just as I did in the thirties and acted just as insane. I didn't think this species existed anymore. I thought they went out with high-button shoes and knickers. But, no—here he was—fifteen years in the same place: Alan Tresser, the last of the old-fashioned toomlers.

He wore a funny red hat with a feather sticking up, a loud funny shirt with wild buttons with different kinds of sayings on the buttons, a whistle around his neck, and screaming, whistling, toomling like crazy—unbelievable in this day and age. Even Lou Goldstein had become a dignified performer, letting loose only during "Simon Sez" games. The Concord Hotel had a toomler for years that they finally had to let go because the business had become too big and lacked the informality necessary for this kind of toomler.

As I stood there I heard Tresser whistle over the loudspeaker and announce, "Paging Judge Crater." He had recognized me and created such a tumult I hid in the corner. He asked me if I could spare ten minutes when he heard about my book. He pulled me into the dining room—it was raining outside and the natives were restless. On the way to the dining room he opened a small closet, so small that only one person could step inside and stand up. "This is my office," he said proudly, with a chuckle. It was full of pictures of Alan with stars through the years, all kinds of crazy signs and props. He showed me some of the signs. "These are some of the crazy activities we announce—they never happen but the people get a laugh out of it. That's all that matters: Bull fighting, kid stabbing, light breathing, gorilla hunt, spear ducking." He showed me the day's menu. On the right side was printed a wonderful luncheon menu with many choices. On the left, "Passover Nutty Sports." (This was the activities program, mimeographed daily.)

Alan Tresser was known as the king of "Simon Sez," despite Lou Goldstein's reputation, who was the best in the business. It was Lou himself who admitted on a Miami radio interview that Alan was the best at the game. Alan claims he started playing the game in 1932 out of sheer necessity. It is said that necessity is the mother of creation and so it was with Alan. He never saw Lou, who started later on the other side of the mountains. He does "Simon Sez" so well that he is the unchallenged king in this game. So much so that the management, each weekend, offered $1,500 to anyone who could last more than five seconds with Alan, and that included the sure-fire line, "Everyone jump up in the air"—and then Simon did not say "Come down."

He's the last of the zanies and although he worked at almost every borscht resort, there were some places who thought him a bit too wild and refused to hire him. He told no jokes, only humorous incidents of actual happenings every day at the resort. He claims there is an inexhaustible amount of such material without repeating.

Here are more nutty and zany activities printed on the daily menus marked "Fallsview Sports—Today's Events"

2:33 Beating your kid over the head with a wet tree.
2:36 Diving from the top of the main building into a bag of hard-boiled eggs.
3:55 Trap shooting: Shoot your big trap off while you are here, but not too often.
5:44 Fly casting. Bring your fly down to the lake. Watch your fly as you cast.

5:55 Chasing butterflies. Better to chase a butterfly than a wild goose, though I haven't seen a wild goose in a long time, or even a plain one.
5:56 Sleeping contest. Try to get some rest here. Take a nap before going to sleep.
Dress for game tonight. Relax in Slax and have fun.
Signed *Tresser, the Simple Simon*
(They tell me that this week has seven full days. Use them.)

And in addition:

2:33 For the Sportswear Association Inc. convention:
Swim a little, skate a little, eat a little, dance with your wife a little, drink a little, hit your kid a little every four minutes. For a large group you do very little littles.
2:35 Try a hike to the card room with a full pack. That ought to keep you busy. First prize: Our entire day camp and two sandpits.
3:00 Lecture by Professor Tresser: "How to use a blackjack on your kid without breaking the blackjack." (Dip it in cement before using.) Take off your kid's hat first. No sense in ruining a good hat.

Day camp events included playing with a nice bobcat, pushing a tree uphill, class in dirty fighting, throwing rusty knives. First prize: a cute gorilla.

Some of the places where he worked were Schawanga, Pines, Lakewood, Green Mansions (after Ernie Glucksman), and Crystal Lake Lodge. Some of the people who worked for him and with him were Gloria Davis, Erwin Corey, Martha Schlamm, Inka Trina, Leon Leshner, Howard DeSylva, Morris Carnofsky. You can tell from these names the kind of performer he was—way out, unorthodox, and different. He still is a rarity in this business.

Alan feels that the trend will never go back to the old days. The public is too demanding and the new generation will never go through what we did in the old days to learn our trade. They want to get there fast. They want instant success and they can get it on TV and a quick hit record.

EDDIE SCHAEFER
How I Stole a Basketball Court

In the early thirties, two weeks before Labor Day at Shady Nook Country Club, Loch Sheldrake, I was second banana on the staff—which means second comic. The owner was a despicable tyrant. One of the things he did was to cut everyone's salary two weeks before Labor Day or slash the staff. Business was always slow. Where could the staff go if they quit? Sometimes salaries were on a sliding scale so that the largest amount was to be paid at the end of the summer. So it was either take the cut or else. I refused to take a cut, so was notified to leave the next day. I decided to get even.

The boss trusted no one, especially toward the end of the season. This owner slept in the lobby. I knew he didn't use his own bedroom. That night I went to the basketball court, took down the basket rings, pulled out the goalposts, took all the balls, the bicycle pump, and even the paint used to paint the lines. Piece by piece, they were carried to the boss's room.

Then I went to my own room to pack my valise and steamer trunk. I remembered that when I first arrived, the sink in my room was cracked and leaking—so I bought another second-hand sink and installed it. Now I proceeded to remove and pack it in my trunk.

On opening the door next morning, the boss was there with two big state policemen. They informed me that they had a warrant against me for stealing a basketball court.

I was taken downtown to court. The judge read the complaint, turned to the boss and said, "You mean to tell me that you accuse this man of stealing an entire basketball court?"

The boss said, "Yes, I accuse him and I vant you should open up his trunk."

The judge looked at me with a sympathetic look and said, "What can I do? You'll have to open the trunk and show him."

The state troopers opened the trunk and out fell the sink. The judge looked with dismay, said, "I've heard of everything, but a sink in a trunk?"

The Millionaire Traffic Cop in Tuxedo, N.Y.

There was a millionaire traffic cop who ran the most notorious speedtrap en route to the Catskills in Tuxedo, N.Y. I was returning from a job in the hills early one morning at 3:00 A.M. when the cop grabbed me. I was back of my car, pushing it. He threatened me with a ticket. At that hour, in order to get rid of him, I slipped him a twenty-dollar bill, folded. It was dark, of course, and I would have loved to see his face when he opened the bill and saw that it was funny money with a picture of Buddy Hackett. (Buddy used to have them printed to give away as a gag.)

The Funeral Car

Jay Jason told me this story, and it's true. A young singer borrowed his father's black funeral car to transport him to the mountains and he gave a lift to other acts. He was thrown out of three places when they saw the car. Charley Rapp, their agent, never found out why.

The staff at Shady Nook were given the worst food. In order to survive, I took an extra job as busboy so I could swipe some extra food. While collecting the dishes on a large tray when the boss wasn't looking, I would pour the remaining milk into a pitcher, move it over to the dishwasher, and drink it. But when I went to drink it, I found that I had poured water into the milk.

The Day I Quarantined the Entire Hotel

The owner always complained that we didn't keep the guests busy enough. Guests complained there was no activity. The boss ordered me to do something—take them away from the hotel for a while, anyplace. So I announced we would take a walk to the secret Indian burial ground. This was our own dump for garbage and burying chicken bones. I took seventy-five people out that day. In order to make the trip exciting and mysterious, I detoured through brush, into the woods, over a stream, through the pasture and hills, and back. The next day the entire hotel broke out with poison ivy and the hotel had to be quarantined.

JACKIE MASON

Jackie Mason (*née* Masler) started his career in the Borscht Belt under most unusual circumstances. He was given his first engagement in the fifties by George Kuttin at a place called Sun Rise Manor, in Ellenville. He walked out on stage and the first words he uttered were: "My God, this place stinks." The boss ran back and threw him out of the hotel.

He was booked into a very orthodox hotel because he was a rabbinical student (he came from a family of rabbis). The name of the hotel was the Pioneer Country Club. He stayed one season. Like many frustrated comics, he always tried to hog the spotlight, even when he served as M.C. to introduce other comedians. He would do a half-hour routine before introducing the star comedian of the show. This, of course, detracted from the comic. Once, while introducing Phil Foster, he did a half hour of Foster. And when he finally introduced Foster, Phil walked out on the stage and said: "How do you do, ladies and gentlemen. You just heard my act—so, good night," and walked off the stage.

Jackie got his first big-time break on the coast with Steve Allen. He was sent there by an agent to replace an act with the Slate Brothers nightclub. Allen caught him there and took a chance with him, even though most people never believed that his strictly Jewish delivery would ever take on TV.

Sullivan heard about him and made him change his routine several times before he gave him an opportunity to appear on the Sullivan show.

I told an agent that this kid would never go anyplace in show business because his entire attitude and delivery were so strictly Jewish, I couldn't see how he could appeal to the vast non-Jewish TV audiences. That shows how wrong I could be.

When Hal Edwards, the agent, met Jackie Mason recently, he reminded him of the first hotel that fired him. Jackie's answer was: "Yes, if they hadn't fired me, I'd still be a social director in the Borscht Belt." Now he earns more than $300,000 a year.

To say that Jackie Mason's career was "kicked off" in the Borscht Belt is putting it correctly but very mildly, for Jackie was actually kicked out of more resort hotels in the Catskills at the beginning of his career than anyone else in show business.

He started as social director for the Pearl Lake Hotel in

Parksville, N.Y., about 1953. His salary was $65 a week but they threw him out after one week's work because he didn't know or care to do the social directing chores. He learned that a social director had to get up at 8:00 A.M. to do calisthenics at 9:00. First of all, he didn't know how to do calisthenics and even if he did, he wouldn't. He was and still is a lazy guy by nature. So why should he do things he didn't want to do if he could get away without doing them? This is still his philosophy.

After being thrown out of his first job, he was discharged from eight more hotels in the next few summers: among them, Fieldstone, Sunrise, Leone Lodge in White Sulpher Springs, Echo Hotel in Ellenville, Hotel Furst in Fallsburgh, etc., etc.

Jack Siegel, the agent, booked him at the Furst Hotel in Fallsburgh and he was discharged after the first week because his material was limited. He had about enough material for one week. He didn't realize that an entertainer can't repeat the same material week after week, especially if many guests stayed for the entire summer. Furthermore, they expected him to organize baseball games, be athletic director, and lead all the daytime activities. He found this not only unpleasant but impossible because he didn't know even how to start a ball game or how to play anything, and frankly he didn't want to.

After a few summers of being fired from one place after another, he found it difficult to get a job—so in order to keep alive, he tried many things. He sold shoes in Gimbels, took odd jobs in different stores. In every case it was the same thing—he wasn't interested in the job and couldn't adapt himself. He just wanted to be a comedian.

At the suggestion of several agents and with the help of Cy Martin, an agent, he collected enough material to go on for half an hour. He went back to Pearl Lake Hotel and held on for the summer.

This was the last Borscht Belt job he held. Cy Martin booked him into about fifty hotels for one-nighters. If they liked him, fine; if not, they didn't have to rebook him. In 1957 he played many club dates and Bar Mitzvahs for many agents, including Henry Stern, Pete Larkin, Jack Siegel, and Cy Martin.

The man most responsible for his big break was Charley Rapp. Pete Larkin recommended him to Charley, who took a liking to him. He not only provided a lot of club dates in the mountains but tried to further his career by recommending him to others and suggesting a good personal manager, Bob Chertog.

Pete Larkin booked him at the Blue Angel club where Mark Leddy saw him, but still thought his act was too Jewish. Then Rapp recommended him to the Slate Brothers nightclub in Los Angeles, where Jan Murray saw him, loved him, and recommended him to Steve Allen, who put him on TV. From there he was made. He went from one big show to another—Gary Moore, Perry Como, Carson, Sullivan, and Jack Paar.

This paragraph was written in 1986 and added to my old Jackie Mason story. He is now appearing in Hollywood at the Canon Theatre, is a tremendous hit, and will be leaving for New York in a few weeks. He has been receiving wonderful reviews on his show "The World According to Me." There is no doubt he will do as well wherever he appears.

In his act he relates the real reason why Ed Sullivan fired him from his show. Jackie had appeared many times with Sullivan and was always a big hit. His style of delivery is unique and includes gestures with his hands and fingers that fit his particular delivery; among these are gestures with his fingers that emphasize jokes.

During one of his appearances with Ed Sullivan way, way back when, he prepared seven or eight minutes of jokes. When Sullivan ran short of time, he would have his director signal to the performer to cut. This happened during one of Jackie's monologues. Jackie, in desperation, made a gesture to the director which he did not mean to be, but which looked obscene (I mean the one in which he uses the middle finger and bends his right arm at the same time). Ed Sullivan was so enraged with Jackie that he not only cancelled his future dates, but was responsible for Jackie being banned from many or all TV shows for some time. He claims to this day that he never meant the gesture to be insulting but it just looked that way.

It was a devastating event in his career and hurt him very much. I am sure that if Ed Sullivan had been more familiar with his style of delivery and had not been so evil-minded, he would not have acted so strongly and hurt Jackie's career so much, for he is a very talented man—one of the first who introduced Jewish humor, along with Myron Cohen, on coast-to-coast TV. He is a brilliant comic.

As this book goes to press, I am happy to add the following to "the trials and tribulations of Jackie Mason." Following his successful Beverly Hills engagement Jackie opened in New York in a large theater and was an instantaneous hit . . . The critics raved, the audience screamed in packed houses. And to top it all off, Jackie Mason was awarded the prestigious Tony Award in 1987 as the BEST COMEDIAN OF THE YEAR.

BENNY LESSEY

Benny Lessey, well-known comedian, started out in the Borscht Belt as a musician. He was a drummer with a band from Brooklyn called Lashinsky's Bluebirds (his real name was Lashinsky), sometimes known as the Tennessee Serenaders. Some of the early places they played were Cherry Hill Farm, the Napanock Country Club, Pinebrook Country Club, Cedars Country Club, Flagler, and Totem Lodge.

He worked in 1925 and 1926 at Totem Lodge. The social director was Charlie Eichels, a schoolteacher. He was known at resorts for producing more performances of "The Student Prince" than Schubert.

Benny left Totem because the boss objected to their running a benefit for the musicians at the end of the summer. They would run a show and dance, then pass the hat around. Katz thought this most undignified, yet when the hat was full, he grabbed it and kept the money.

He remembers when Katz tried to be his own architect—designing new buildings. Katz would stand over the dirt with a stick in his hand, the carpenters around him, marking his plans in the dirt. If he didn't like it, a brush of the foot would eradicate the design.

He recalls those overnight boat trips to Albany on the Hudson River Night Line. It was as exciting an event as an ocean crossing on the *Queen Mary*.

The social director (toomler) was usually broke before the summer job because of an unemployed winter and had to borrow money for clothes and other necessities. He usually had to go to a loan shark and pay $600 for $500. The shylock would give the money willingly enough, making sure he got his hundred first. He would see the social director off for the summer, saying, "Take care of yourself. Drink lots of malted milks and drive slowly. Send money." He couldn't afford valises, so carried his belongings in overnight Manischevitz (Matzo) boxes.

There was always the practical joker electrician. He used to put his finger in a hot socket and tell the staff it wasn't on. Then when the staff member tried it, he would be thrown five feet in the air by the shock.

DAN SHAPIRO

Dan Shapiro is one of the best-known comedy and song writers in the business today. He contributed comedy material for almost every big name in show business, including Jackie Gleason, Tony Martin, and Milton Berle among others. He was born in 1910 and started his show business career as a social director in the Catskills at the age of 16. My interview with him brought out many points we have touched on and several new angles that I think might be of interest.

Danny started, as many of the social directors did, as a musician in a small band known as the Hollywood Ramblers. They came from the Bronx. The leader was Irving Haber, now owner of the Upstairs and Downstairs nightclub in New York City. Their first job was at the Lakeshore Hotel in Kiamesha Lake, N.Y. At first it was an audition for Memorial Day. Many hotel owners got free entertainment and music by asking bands and entertainers to audition for the holiday. If they did well, they had a summer job.

The band traveled over the Hudson on the ferry to Weehauken and took a miserable New Jersey train to the Catskills. The trip of only 100 miles took five hours. They arrived covered from train soot. After the audition, the boss replied, "The music was all right, but I don't like the musicians—they're too heavy. They eat too much. Get me some thin musicians and you're hired." Danny promised the boss the fat boys would go on a diet so that by July 1st they would be skinnier. He got the job.

Danny was the toomler in the band. He made the jokes and gags and kept toomling during the day. Members received the big salary of ten dollars per week plus board.

That was the birth of the social director, the toomler, the life of the party. Many of our present comedians started that way.

The next summer Danny told the owner he was interested in the social director's job instead of playing in the band. The boss reluctantly agreed to pay him $10 per week, as before. The boss made up for the social director's salary, which Danny found out after the season. There were several kochaleins (also called *kochelefels*) vacationing in a nearby bungalow colony consisting of families. The boss made a deal with them at five dollars per family—they would have the privilege of watching the shows on Friday and Saturday. There were 20 to 40 families. The boss collected sometimes as much as $500 per season for the services of the social director and yet paid him only $10 per week.

In those days there was no staff in the small hotels—just a small band and the social director. It was his job to pick out talent from among the guests and furnish material. Danny was not an entertainer but he could tell a story and write funny parodies to the hit songs of the day, such as "Roll Out the Bagel." In his constant search for new material, he lifted much material from Broadway shows. The clientel was an older Jewish crowd who seldom went to Broadway shows, so the material was not familiar. One of the best productions Danny put on was a miniature of the "Jazz Singer."

A humorous incident about this play is worth retelling. Danny found his talent wherever he could. The highly dramatic finish to the "Jazz Singer" needed someone to sing "Kol Nidre." Danny, who played the lead, could not sing. He discovered the *shochet* (chicken slaughter) in the market was also a part-time cantor. He made a deal with him to sing "Kol Nidre" as Danny mouthed it at the finale, for ten dollars, The boss didn't know about it. Danny figured the boss would be so pleased with the show he wouldn't object.

The show started and did well. The time near the finale came when Danny, as the lead, was in the synagogue and ready to sing "Kol Nidre" in his dying father's place. The cantor stood offstage waiting for his cue to sing. He was enthralled with the performance. Suddenly the boss came backstage and yelled to the cantor, "What da hell are you doing back here?"

"I was hired to sing 'Kol Nidre' by Danny for ten dollars."

"Ten dollars?" screamed the owner. "Are you crazy? I pay Danny ten dollars a week—why should I pay you. Get the hell out of here." With that he threw the cantor off the stage. Came the great moment for singing of "Kol Nidre," and Danny started mouthing the words. No voice came from offstage. Once again Danny started. Then noticing no one there, he coughed and cried out to the audience, "Damn that laryngitis again." Curtain.

There was an era during the early thirties when front page headlines featured the finding of several gangster bodies, encased in cement, sunk at the bottom of beautiful Catskill Mountain lakes—Kamiesha, Swan Lake , etc.

The mob of Murder Inc. and other New York gangsters used to send their wives, families and many times their girlfriends up to the Catskills for the summer on long vacations. They paid the owner double for the privilege and actually took over the place. They received the red carpet treatment and anything they did was okay. The social director and staff were warned never to make a play for any girls for fear that they might turn out to be a mobsters' molls.

Danny and his assistant took a row on the lake one day and stumbled upon a floating body which had been dislodged from its cement foundation. It was not unusual to see the mob shooting at passing cars' tires. If someone had the urge to ride a horse into the lobby for laughs, it was done. . . . until the police found several bodies floating in the lakes. Then the mob had to change their locale to a less noticeable vacation spot.

In their constant search for something different to present to the guests, the social directors stooped to all kinds of devices and ideas. Once during a long rainy spell (this is the worst crisis at any resort), Danny announced that after dinner something different would take place on the veranda. He announced that each guest should take a pencil and paper and describe what rain means. The answers were surprising. "Rain is wet. Rain is dreary. Rain brings flowers." Anyway, a couple of hours were killed. It was called a Rain Analysis Contest.

The Borscht Belt uncovered talent of all kinds—singers, comedians, actors, writers, producers and artists. It afforded them a chance to show their talents and develop into fine artists and achieve recognition. The alumni list of the Borscht Belt speaks for itself.

In the beginning, the owners never considered that entertainment was important. The food department came first. They were practically forced into show business. Most hotel owners, then, regarded the expense for music and entertainers "a roise gevarfen the gelt," which means the money is thrown out.

It was a great opportunity for talent. Where else could entertainers work before audiences without restraint and experiment with ideas? Nowadays performers have to make it with a record or TV exposure without any chance for experience, which only time can bring.

Jewish parodies written around the hits of the day were always a sure fire hit with Borscht Belt audiences. Allan Sherman, one of the biggest record-selling artists, made his success by writing and singing parodies to famous melodies with a Jewish flavor.

Most social directors entertaining Jewish audiences had to learn Jewish expressions. Some were brought up in the East Side's poor neighborhood and this came naturally to them. As they improved from this experience, they refined this style, and so were born many famous comedians such as Sam Levinson, Jackie Mason, and Henny Youngman. They changed their material when they became better known and entertained audiences of all kinds throughout the country.

In the old days the owner would charge a small fee to visiting kocheleins or farm guests to come to their big shows on Saturdays. Nowadays, as a noticeable parallel, big hotels in Florida and elsewhere encourage bus tours to come in large groups to watch their big star shows. It helps defray heavy expenses.

JAN MURRAY

This is a true story of how Jan Murray, one of our leading comedians today, got his start in show business, in the Borscht Belt, as told to me by George Kuttin, the agent.

Cohen, the owner of the Stanley Hotel in Lakewood, fired his comedian and called George Kuttin for a quick replacement. Comedians in those days congregated in a drug store on West 46th Street. Kuttin went down to find a comedian quickly. He was unsuccessful—none were available. When he returned to his office, a skinny, broken-down-looking tall, lanky young fellow by the name of Murray Janowsky walked in. He said he heard Kuttin was looking for a comic. Kuttin asked him what experience he had. He answered, nothing, just entertainment at bar mitzvahs and weddings. Kuttin, in desperation, told him to wait at home, packed, and if he didn't hear from him by 4 P.M. that afternoon, forget it.

By four, Kuttin was still unable to find a comic, so in desperation he called Murray and told him to get on the bus and rush down to the Stanley Hotel in Lakewood. At 6 P.M. he got a phone call from Cohen, the owner, who screamed, "What the hell did you send me, an inexperienced, broken-down, skinny kid. I thought he was a busboy and sent him in the kitchen."

Kuttin pleaded with him to give him a chance. In desperation the owner made him dress neatly, lent him a suit and put him on. He was an instant success.

The next week when Kuttin came down to Lakewood to visit the hotel owner, there was Jan Murray with a new suit, a new tuxedo and a new name, well entrenched in his new job as Social Director at the Stanley Hotel.

DICK SHAWN

April 23rd, 1987, was one of the happiest birthdays in my life for I had just signed my contract with my publisher George Blagowidow of Hippocrene Books for my autobiography *Music in My Heart and Borscht in My Blood.* But near the end of my birthday I heard news on the radio and TV that shocked me and the world of entertainment. . . . DICK SHAWN, one of our greatest comedians, and a good friend had just died. . . .

I was greatly affected by this sad news for I remembered when I first met Dick an unknown comedian in 1952 and booked him to appear at the resort Totem Lodge. . . . He was such a big hit, so original, so unique, so different and so funny—he had the audience rolling in the aisles.

The next day I called my friend Harry Kalcheim of the William Morris Agency and suggested he sign him up right away. I raved about his talents, his act and predicted stardom for him. The William Morris Agency signed him and he was on his way. But to my surprise and disappointment nothing happened with him for a few years. When I inquired about him the Morris Agency told me that he truly was an unusual and great talent but somehow he would not take the advice of his agent and turned down important big-money engagements and chose to appear in small unknown, off Broadway shows.

He was an artistic genius who chose to do it his own way and because of that he never became the important star I had predicted and hoped for. I appeared with him at many benefits and he was always the hit of the show.

After reading all the accolades and eulogies, especially from his friends at the Friars Club, who incidentally filled three buses to attend his funeral services, I finally chose the following articles that best described Dick Shawn and his talents. The first was written by Charles Champlin, Entertainment Editor of the *L.A. Times;* the other, written by his friend and former agent Rabbi Jerry Cutler and

printed in the "Bintel Brief" of his synagogue, "the Sholom Aleichem Temple of Creative Arts. They kindly gave me permission to
reprint them.

Dick Shawn: Surreal Exit to a Unique Career

By CHARLES CHAMPLIN
Times Arts Editor

It was the last uniquenes of a unique career that Dick Shawn
could fall dying on stage in full view of an audience that
imagined, for some long, uncomfortable moments, that the fall
was part of his act.

But Shawn, who did fall and die during a performance in San
Diego last week, at the age of 57, used to lie on stage
throughout the intermission of his one-man show, "The Second
Greatest Entertainer in the Whole Wide World." He would be
partly covered by crumpled newspapers, for reasons that now
escape me.

Stagehands tidied up and changed the set around him, and
when the intermission was over, Shawn would arise, dust
himself off and carry on. It was as surrealistic as everything else
about his show, and even in the best of times that bit caused a
small shiver of anxiety in some of his viewers.

In San Diego, the fall preceded the intermission, and an
audience could easily be forgiven for not sensing at once that
comedy had segued into tragedy.

If we can assume that there are good and bad ways to go,
leaving in full stride when the act is proceeding well must rank
with the better ways.

The truth is that Dick Shawn for years had seemed so richly
varied a talent that his problem was to find material as good as
he was. He had a wonderful, original, spiky and erratic
intelligence that could not be satisfied with one-liners and
routines, or even the fine impressions he was capable of.

But eventually he had, in the very best sense of the term, got
his act together. This was, I suppose, a half-dozen or more years
ago. He played it in Los Angeles, took it on the road and in 1985
brought it back to Los Angeles, honed to perfection, and
enjoyed an unusually long run at the Canon Theatre, in a town
that does not support long runs easily.

What Shawn did was not easy to describe. It was a seemingly free-associative skein of bits, thoughts, and actions. It was a comedy about comedy, a performance about performance and the performer's peculiar relationship with his audiences. And it was, finally, a kind of acted-out speculation on the reality of the absurd and the absurdity of much of what we think of as reality.

In summary, it sounds pretentious, but it never was, because Shawn was a consummate entertainer, actor, comedian, singer, dancer, mime and mimic. Then, too, he had been in the trenches or on the boards so long that he knew how to play audiences like a mighty Wurlitzer, to their complete satisfaction. He even embroiled them in his act, a procedure fraught with peril in lesser hands.

He was a very funny man, but the deeper appeal of the one-man show he had built out of his life was that he seemed, even on the several dozenth performance of the material, speculative and rather vulnerable. It was as if the small miracle of communication with an audience was striking him afresh, even as you watched, and there was charm and poignancy in it.

Shawn's last audience will be hard put to remember anything but the unsettling reality of the fall and the long and puzzling wait. The rest of us can think back to the act that was, with the model airplane, the banana and the oranges and the crumpled newspapers, and wonder if the marvelous Dick Shawn had had some last, surprised and resigned sense that absurdity and reality were merging into one.

Rabbi's Message

I heard it over the radio. "Dick Shawn is dead . . ." Like everyone else who heard the shocking news, I refused to believe it. Dick Shawn, the most creative, animated, exciting, imaginative comedian of his era dead? No way! The battery of a car not turning over . . . is dead. A microphone with a blown fuse . . . is dead. A short wave radio, a vacuum cleaner, an electric shaver, those things die. Not entertainers of the caliber of Dick Shawn.

Over thirty years ago when I accepted my first job as a social director at the Royal Hotel in Mountaindale, N.Y., I chose Shawn's classic, "Massah Richard" as my first routine. It did great and why not, I stole it from the greatest.

Years later, I moved to Los Angeles. At the time, I was producing "Room Service" at the Edison Theatre in New York. The star, Ron Leibman, was leaving to do a film, "Where's Poppa", in Hollywood. A replacement was needed. I forwarded the name of Dick Shawn, my associate producers loved it. I flew back and negotiated a deal with Dick and his agent.

It was during the summer months when all the shows habitually do poorly. "You're not going to close the show soon, are you?" Dick asked. I gave him my word that we will continue its run indefinitely and took off for California. He went into rehearsal and opened in two weeks, the very same night my partners posted 'closing' notices. I severed my relationships with my two partners and was too embarrassed to talk to Shawn. Some years later, now a rabbi at the Sholom Aleichem Temple of Creative Arts, a roast was held in my honor. "Would I ask Dick Shawn?" "No, but if someone else wants to, it's okay with me."

He was asked. He said he would be in Palm Springs for an afternoon show, if he could manage a way to be there, he would. I held out no hope whatsoever.

The evening started. Red Buttons, Ed Asner, Marty Allen, Jackie Vernon, Stanley Myron Handelman, Jackie Kahane, Louis Quinn, Sid Miller . . . no Shawn. Not surprising. Half way through, this white haired shtarka breezed past me and took a seat on the dais. He was brilliant, absolutely brilliant. And, he never once mentioned New York.

Not long ago he called me. The Friar's were going to roast him at one of their raunchy stags. "I need a benediction," he told me. Dick Shawn delivering a benediction to his fellow comics after they have verbally abused him for two hours? Has he mellowed? Is this the same Dick Shawn I knew and loved? The one who was liable to do anything on stage so long as it was the furthest thing from any normal person's mind. A benediction? I gave him a standard benediction and he thanked me. "Oh yes," he said before he hung up, "one more thing, I want to know how you like it. I'm going to take a mouthful of pea soup and when I go out and thank everyone I'm going to throw up over everybody." I screamed with laughter . . . so did everyone else, I'm told, who attended the roast.

During my last conversation with him a few weeks ago, I asked him for something in relationship to food I could use in an updated version of my "Celebrity Kosher Cookbook." He told me that as a kid he didn't smoke, drink or run around with women. Growing up he never had fried or fat foods or canned juices. He used to carry carrots and celery and raw eggs wherever he went. "When I was forty and all my friends who indulged in all of those things were going downhill, I said, that's it! Now it's going to be greasy hamburgers and smoking and drinking and cavorting. I was going to find out what I missed. I'm having a great time!"

Dear friend Dick, thank you for all those great times you gave to all of us.

Rabbi Jerry Cutler

GENE BARRY

Gene Barry, of Bat Masterson and Burke's Law TV fame, was born Eugene Klass in the 116th Street Harlem section of New York City. When he finished high school at the age of seventeen, he decided on a show business career and heard that the Borscht Belt was a good place to start.

He went to Henry Stern, the Catskill booker, and was interviewed by the owner of a small hotel in Woodridge called "Lyndy's." When the owner asked what his experiences were, he lied and mentioned working at the Paramount, Capitol, Palace, and Loew's State. He forgot to add "as usher."

The owner said, "You look like the boy for me. I'll give you $15 a week and room and board."

Gene Barry, who had picked his new name out of a book for professional purposes, wanted to sound professional so he asked if there was a stage at the hotel.

"Of course," said the owner. "Vat a qvestion. Ve have a beautiful stage with a long approaching staircase and chandeliers. You do three shows for Fourth of July, one dramatic show on Friday, one vaudeville on Saturday, and an original revue on Sunday. Also a little entertainment during SARPER. Gene quickly agreed even though he didn't understand what SARPER (supper) meant.

Elated, he borrowed $25 from his uncle to buy a white suit (standard equipment for a social director) and pay for his fare, borrowed a valise from another relative, and off he went to the mountains. When he arrived at Lyndy's, he found to his dismay that the stage was the first landing of the staircase leading upstairs from the lobby and the chandelier was the lobby lights. He knocked himself out for three days and nights and when it was over, the owner called him aside and quietly said, "I don't think you're the boy for me," gave him $7.50 (which was one-half the week's wages, pro rata), and fired him on the spot. This was the beginning of Gene Barry's career in show business.

PHIL SILVERS

During the summer of 1932 at Totem Lodge, Benny Lessey, Joey Faye, and Snag Werris, who were my comedians on the staff, told me that they thought they could get their friends Phil Silvers and Rags Ragland to come up some weekend as our guests and perhaps perform for just laughs and expenses. The boss was always looking to get talent for free, so he consented and I told the boys to go ahead.

Phil Silvers and Rags Ragland had been top bananas in burlesque. Joey Faye had played with them several seasons, so they were familiar with every well-known burlesque bit. This meant time saving and no rehearsals for sketches. They could put on all the sketches by themselves without my worrying. I was happy.

The weekend they arrived was a wild one, for these boys were not only toomlers and funny guys, but were terrific "Chasers" (ladies men). I was always a nervous guy and when our show was produced on Saturday night, my nerves were at their height, for this was a culmination of a full week's work—after rehearsing musical numbers, openings, etc., etc. The comedians, all of them, Phil Silvers, Rags Ragland, Benny Lessey, Joey Faye, and Julie Oshins, were practical jokesters but I was too busy to realize this.

Just before curtain time on Saturday night, I was running around like crazy checking everything, when suddenly Phil Silvers yelled, "Hold it!"

I asked frantically, "What's the matter?"

He yelled, "We lost the Sassafram." (This was doubletalk and meant nothing.)

Ordinarily under normal circumstances, I might have recognized the doubletalk but now I was frantic. I gave instructions to hold the curtain, delay the overture and everyone look for the Sassafram. They searched high and low and delayed the curtain for almost fifteen minutes. Everyone was in on the joke but me. Finally they yelled, "Okay, we found it."

Relieved, I said, "Okay, on with the show." It was sometime after that I found out the joke was on me. Phil Silvers and the boys kept laughing about it for years.

MY FRIENDS SAUL TURTELTAUB AND LEONARD KOROBKIN

This story was written on March 8, 1979. Saul is presently one of the leading, successful television producers and writers in Hollywood. He is responsible for such hits as "Sanford and Son," "What's Happening," "Carter Country," Dick Van Dyke, Jackie Gleason, Marlo Thomas, and many others. Leonard Korobkin has become one of the most successful theatrical and music attorneys on the coast. They both started with me at Totem Lodge way back in 1951.

I had served as social director at Totem Lodge for more than ten summers and was getting tired of doing all the work myself. I prevailed upon Mr. Katz to let me hire a few assistants.

He reluctantly agreed, providing the price was right. One day while sitting in the Totem Lodge office before the summer, in walked a skinny tall, wild-looking character with a short, bespectacled, studious-looking guy. "What can I do for you?" I asked them.

The tall guy said, "We're a comedy team. My name is Saul Turteltaub and this is my partner and straight man Leonard Korobkin."

"I never heard of you," I replied, very doubtful that they could fill my requirements, although Saul looked something like the nervous, pimple-faced guy I was years ago. "Make me laugh," I said, very challenging.

The big guy took off his shirt and pants in a flash and there, under his clothes, was a Flash Gordon Superman costume. He started jumping up and down the seats and desk and climbing the walls while his partner just looked on and laughed. I never saw anyone act so crazy in front of a possible employer, so I laughed harder and said a few unimportant things like, "We don't pay much, but if you want to work hard and learn show business, I'll be glad to help you." We agreed on a ridiculous price, for Saul was very persuasive.

"Mr. Tobias," he said, "I heard of your wonderful reputation in the resort business and we are anxious to work with you and learn as much as possible." I hired them, for I knew the money was so small, Katz would not object.

The first thing I told them, and this was my biggest mistake, "Boys, your names don't sound right for show business comedians. Who's gonna remember Saul Turteltaub and Leonard Korobkin? Let's change to names that sound easy and are easy to remember. How about Stan Taylor for you, Saul, and Lenny Corbett for you, Korobkin?" They willingly agreed, for the job was important to them.

At that time it was almost Memorial Day and Katz always tried to get some of the help to come up early so they could do some of the dirty work, like painting bungalows and fixing boats.

I suggested, "How would you boys like to come up to Totem two weeks before Memorial Day and enjoy the outdoor living, sunshine, and have some fun?" They were available and quickly agreed. Little did they know what was going to happen. As soon as they arrived on the bus, Katz gave them brushes and paint and overalls, and put them to work painting and fixing . . . especially the new boats. They worked harder than laborers and by the time the season opened, they were exhausted.

However, they never regretted taking the job, for I willingly let them use my joke file and they spent much time in the social hall where they lived, typing and lifting my material. To show their appreciation, when my wife Sophie arrived, they built a fire around our bungalow as an Indian sign of welcome and friendship. They scared the hell out of my wife and daughter. Suffice it to say it was the beginning of a long and lasting friendship which still exists. I would be remiss if I did not state here that Leonard Korobkin has done more for me in handling my business since I moved to California in 1972 than anyone else I know. I am most grateful and appreciative for both their friendships through the years.

I was invited by Jerry Cutler (Rabbi) and Charles Powell, (President) of the Synagogue of Performing Arts to appear on their program called "The Borscht Belt" as a surprise guest artist. I have been a member of this synagogue since arriving in California, at the suggestion of Saul Turteltaub, who was the first president and founder.

When I arrived at the show, I was told by Charlie Powell that I could only do five minutes, so I decided to do my "Guess the Real Name of the Star" routine from my book.

Saul was in the audience with his wife, so I thought I would play a joke on him and see if he would recognize his old name. After telling the real names of some of the stars, I asked the audience, "Who is Stan Taylor today?"

Saul Turteltaub recognized the name immediately and yelled out, "That's me, Saul Turteltaub." The audience was surprised to hear their former president admit that he once used another name, for since arriving in California Saul had used his real name and gave up Stan Taylor as soon as he left Totem Lodge.

Of course, I had to explain to the audience how it had all happened at Totem.

Chapter 8

Hotels And Owners

I worked at Totem Lodge from 1927 to 1938. After twelve years in the same place I thought it was time for a change. I remembered that Jennie Grossinger had once told me that any time I decided to make a change, she would love to have me work for her. One day after the 1938 summer season was over, I saw that it was useless trying to convince Mr. Katz I deserved another raise. I called Jennie on the phone and told her I wanted to leave Totem. She immediately hired me on the phone and told me to work out details with her representative, Milton Blackstone, who was Grossinger's advertising and public relations man.

GROSSINGER'S

What a difference it was dealing with Jennie Grossinger as opposed to dealing with Katz. While I had to sweat each year negotiating my

117

contract at Totem Lodge, I found my negotiations with Grossinger so simple and easy and quick. I met with Blackstone, the price was agreed, a memo made and before I knew it, I was on my way to Grossinger's for the Passover holidays of 1939.

However, I found it was quite a change working at Grossinger's as compared with Totem Lodge. At Totem I was practically a one-man organization: hiring help, writing and directing the show, acting as master of ceremonies, leading the band, and toomling the guests during the day. In addition, I was director of activities, booker of the talent, and also performing myself in every department. I was happy doing all these things because that's the kind of guy I am.

I therefore felt let down when I found upon arriving at Grossinger's that I was an extra wheel in an already well-oiled and successfully operating machine. It was such a large organization, built up over the years, that I found it difficult to adjust myself and get started. Although my contract read that I was to be program director and director of activities, I found the setup so complete that it was impossible to display any of my talents or abilities. The staff who had been there for years resented a new, young, ambitious punk. The acts were booked by Milton Blackstone (manager of Eddie Fisher, who started at Grossinger's); the shows M.C.'d by Billy Reed (later owner of Billy Reed's Little Club). The daytime activities were under the capable supervision of Abe Sharkey; the orchestra was under the leadership of Zinn Arthur (who later became assistant to Josh Logan). I even found it difficult to talk to Jennie Grossinger.

Despite the pleasant surroundings, wonderful management, good pay, swell people to work with, I was unhappy because I couldn't do what I was hired to do. I felt that I must have been hired for my name, reputation, and guest following rather than actually for my talents. I prevailed on Milton Blackstone to allow me to put on an original staff show. He finally consented to let me do this in the middle of the week.

I threw the book at them, took all my best material collected through the years. It was a tremendous success, so great that Jennie insisted we repeat it on the following Saturday night and several times thereafter. In fact the next season she asked my permission to do the show annually with her staff, which I gladly granted. She was the only one I knew who would give credit for material where it belonged. Others took my material, presented it each summer, and sometimes when I hired them on the staff, they would tell me that other people took credit for my material. So I finally decided to publish a book in 1958 called "How to Produce an Amateur Show." I figured I might as well collect for some of my material, which I did.

At the end of the summer Jennie Grossinger told me she was pleased with my services and offered me a deal for the following summer. I graciously refused for I knew that this was not for me. I would rather be a big man in a smaller hotel than a small guy at Grossinger's. I left Grossinger's after only one summer, with regrets, for never have I ever worked for such nice people. Sometimes when I received my salary check I felt guilty and ashamed to take it. But I honestly was not happy being a figurehead. I had to be a working boss. I found that at Grossinger's there were too many Indian chiefs and not enough Indians. I guess the capacity and the immensity of Grossinger's made it possible to carry such a large staff.

For instance, there were a dozen college basketball players, All-American collegiate stars, sitting around all week doing nothing but waiting for that one game on Friday night. They also had a complete dramatic staff, including Phil Foster, who started at Grossinger's in 1939 as a dramatic actor. It was I who took him out of the dramatic shows, wrote some material for him as a comedian, and gave him his first opportunity in our midweek vaudeville show. The room and board expenses for the staff alone were tremendous and only a large hotel like Grossinger's could afford them.

The reason basketball was played on Friday night was for religious reasons. In those days Grossinger's was a kosher hotel, and Pa and Ma Grossinger were orthodox. No music, dancing, or shows could be presented indoors on Friday night, so basketball was its substitute until big college basketball eliminated this activity.

As for carrying large dramatic staffs for one show a week, this too was eliminated and a traveling dramatic group, such as Stanley Wolf Players, was substituted.

Art Buchwald

Art Buchwald once wrote the following in his column:

> Grossinger's is not just a resort. It's a way of life. From morning until night the guests are coddled, amused, lectured, and entertained. There is nothing Grossinger's won't do for a guest.

MUSIC IN MY HEART

The first person we met when we arrived at Grossinger's was Lou Goldstein, who is in charge of all guest activities. We noticed that Grossinger's had golf courses, tennis courts, volleyball, bowling alleys, swimming pools, etc. and since we've been active in Pierre Salinger's Anti-Physical Fitness Program, we became a little nervous. But Mr. Goldstein assured us that the athletic facilities had nothing to do with the guests. "We put them there," he said, "because we have a lot of land we don't know what to do with. If you're like the other guests, you won't be on your feet more than ten minutes the entire day."

"Well, what do you do then?" we asked.

"In the morning you sit down for breakfast in the dining room. Then you walk—all downhill—to the terrace where I put on an hour's show of jokes and laughs. After the show there is calisthenics. I give finger exercises for people who are going to play gin rummy and canasta in the afternoon.

"Then I hold up a three-pound medicine ball and let each person touch it."

"What happens next?" we asked excitedly.

"Then you rest up for the walk to a couch in the lobby where you prepare yourself for the most strenuous activity of the day—which is eating lunch. After lunch, if you're not tired and don't want to take a nap, you go to the pool where you sit in a chaise lounge while we put on a diving show for you. Not everyone likes to watch it because you have to move your head up and down. When the show is over, we all go over to the dance studio to sit and watch a dance lesson.

"Then you go back to your couch in the lobby to rest up before going upstairs to change for dinner. After sitting in the cocktail lounge, you sit in the dining room and then you go into the nightclub and sit and watch the show."

"That's very nice," we said. "Pierre Salinger would give this hotel a very good rating."

"Of course," Mr. Goldstein said, "there are some physical fitness fanatics here too and we're at their service. For instance, if you want to play horseshoes, all you do is throw the horseshoe. One of our staff picks it up for you, cleans it, and hands it back to you. All you have to do is throw it again.

"If you want to play ping pong and you feel it's too exhausting, we'll remove the net.

"If you want to play baseball, your busboy will run the bases for you."

"You've sold me," we said.

"We believe in catering to the guests," he said.

"Unfortunately, the more activities you have for the guests, the more spoiled they become. A few weeks ago, on the day of the eclipse, a lady came outside and saw it was very cloudy, and she said to me, 'Mr. Goldstein, are you going to cancel the eclipse today?'"

The King of the Toomlers, Lou Goldstein of Grossinger's, has become famous because of his Simon Sez game. When people check into Grossinger's, they don't even ask for him by name. They say, "Where's Simon?" One lady asked him once, "Tell me, Simon, when are you going to write about how you play 'Simon Sez' like other comedians so that I can buy the book and give it to my friends so they can play Simon Sez like you do." "I don't write jokes or books like other comedians but maybe someday they will write about my Simon Sez—posthumously." And the lady replied: "Good. Please make it soon."

Lou says the Simon Sez reputation is driving him crazy. Some men can hang up shingles when they become doctors, lawyers, or accountants, but Lou is just known as Simon. Recently he checked into a hotel in Miami Beach and an elderly gentleman walked up to him and said, "Simon, you have brought me such pleasure and entertainment during my visits to Grossinger's, I would like to do something for you. My Cadillac is standing outside. Treat it like yours." Simon did—he sold it.

During one of his visits to Miami Beach, Simon parked his car in a lot and an old lady who recognized him but couldn't remember his name, yelled at the top of her voice, "Yoo hoo, Simple. . . ."

Although Lou Goldstein has become famous because of his inimitable presentation of Simon Sez, nevertheless he has developed into a wonderful humorist and his supply of material is unlimited. It must be, in order to keep entertaining crowds all year round and many times the same audience. So he varies his material. Sometimes before his Simon Sez game, which is always the big finish, he tells gags and does comedy routines. (He has a great field for obtaining new material; what with every known comedian appearing at Grossinger's year in and year out, Lou has been able to amass the greatest and best collection of comedy material in the business.)

He tells stories about child psychology, Jewish humor, marriage; every conceivable type of story is on the tip of his tongue.

His crowning glory and happiest day in memory is when he was married recently at Grossinger's. They put on a wedding for him that was worth ten to fifteen thousand dollars. They invited hundreds of guests and everything was free of charge. Lou says they had to when he told Jennie Grossinger that he got a better offer from "dorten." (This is what he calls the Concord Hotel, their biggest competitor. It is against the rules to mention the name of the Concord at Grossinger's, so it is "dorten," meaning some other place.)

The bigget laugh he ever heard in his life came from a rabbi. It was the well-known Rabbi Harry Stone who married Lou Goldstein and his bride. The audience was full of celebrities in every field. As the glass was placed on the floor for Lou to step on, indicating completion of the ceremony, Lou stepped on the glass and the rabbi stepped up to the microphone and proclaimed: "Simon Sez you are now married."

Lou is in great demand with his routines, especially Simon Sez, throughout the country. Recently, on coast-to-coast TV, he conducted Simon Sez games and contests for a nationwide audience. He admits that I was the one responsible for him going on "Be My Guest," a CBC TV show several years ago.

George Bennet worked at Grossinger's as publicity and public relations man from 1948 to 1956. He was originally hired by Milton Blackstone and when he left that resort, he was not on speaking terms with Milton and hasn't spoken to him since. The reasons, he says, were personal.

At the time he started, Grossinger's had just begun to break into the press and big news with the start of Barney Ross's training. Celebrities such as Eddie Cantor, Milton Berle, Sophie Tucker, and some columnists were brought up to Grossinger's by Blackstone.

It was Bennet's job to widen the scope of publicity and try to attract people from all over the country, not only New York and the East. Bennet had a good newspaper background, having been in charge of public relations for David O. Selznick movie stars and well-known industrial firms. It was Ted Baldwin who recommended him to Blackstone.

In order to widen the scope of publicity and potential guests, his first job was to create travel agencies all over the country, which they never had before. He did this by visiting forty cities during the cold winter and meeting travel agents personally. In three years he increased the business from out-of-state visitors from 7,000 to 250,000 per year.

His job was to create excitement in the news by bringing stars of every field of endeavor for they generate news and publicity at the hotel they visit. People like to return home and brag about the celebrities they met at Grossinger's.

Some of the names he was personally responsible for attracting to Grossinger's were Rocky Marciano (whom he befriended before he became champion and who reciprocated this kindness when he won the title; he refused every place else but Grossinger's.) Other names he attracted were Kim Novak, Tuesday Weld, Jayne Mansfield, Joe DiMaggio, Jersey Joe Walcott, Dennis James, Joey Bishop, Tony Randall, Herman Wauk, Earl Wilson, chess champion Bobby Fisher; ball players Billy Pierce, Yogi Berra, Don Larsen, and others.

He tried to attract out-of-town sport celebrities so that when they visited Grossinger's, he could take pictures of them in action at play with guests and send the pictures to the local papers who always printed them, thus giving Grossinger's out-of-town publicity and prestige and more guests.

He was always careful not to emphasize the "Borscht Belt" image to out-of-town Gentile guests whom he tried to attract. The Gentiles always thought that the Borscht Circuit, including Grossinger's, was a place where fat, sloppy women and little fat men in shorts with protruding bellies ran around boisterously, and in the evening displayed their diamonds and bragged about their wealth. They were surprised to find that the Jews who visited Grossinger's were all very refined, nice people, the finest; the kind they found at home at their country club. When they saw all that the Borscht Belt had to offer in the way of food and entertainment, they realized that this was the best vacation buy in the business, and so they started to visit Grossinger's, no matter what their color or creed.

The image was changed. The owners were searching for respectability and wanted to change the image of the Borscht Belt. It was the public relations agents' job to do so and they surely did a wonderful job, especially George Bennet. Golf, tennis, and all the finest things in life became the outstanding attractions at Grossinger's and at all the best Borscht Belt hotels. No wonder the owners were trying to eliminate the name "Borscht Belt." But it has become synonymous with the best in life and vacation pleasures and certainly should not be considered any longer in any derogatory manner.

The True Story of How Eddie Fisher Was Discovered

So many stories have been told about Eddie Fisher's discovery at Grossinger's, that I finally asked Milton Blackstone for the true story, and here it is:

Eddie Cantor had been a constant visitor, guest and part of the family at Grossinger's for many years. One day he told Milton Blackstone that he'd like to do a complete show at Grossinger's the next Decoration Day. He was booked for a long tour ahead and felt this would be a good spot to break in the show. Milton was elated. He suggested that Eddie might use a youngster with a great voice who was singing with the band—named Eddie Fisher.

"No, thanks. You do your show and I'll do mine."

Milton Blackstone said nothing but figured out a sure way of letting Cantor hear Fisher. The day ahead he asked Cantor what time he wanted to rehearse. Eddie said 5:00 P.M. would be fine.

Blackstone made sure that the next day at 4:45 Eddie Fisher was on the stage rehearsing his act. When Cantor walked into the hall at 5:00, there was Fisher. After hearing him, Cantor was tremendously impressed and told Milton that he would introduce Fisher personally to the Grossinger audience that night. He did so and Eddie Fisher was an instant success. After Fisher's last song, Cantor asked him in front of the audience of 1,000 people: "How would you like to join my company on a cross-country tour?" The rest is history.

Prediction of Things to Come

I spoke with Milton Blackstone for a long time, told him how impressed I was with what I saw in the Catskills over the weekend while visiting 13 hotels, and complimented him as the man most responsible for the success of Grossinger's Hotel. It was Grossinger's and the Concord that set the pace for the entire Catskill Mountain resorts. To my surprise, Milton said, "If you think they have been building rapidly and improving, wait until you see what happens in the next few years. This is only the beginning for all of them."

I said, "What do you mean? How much further can they go? Most of them are already in hock over their heads. Comes the first bad year—POW—bankruptcy. Most of the hotels will be owned by the banks, who are in turn owned by most of the big hotel owners. So it will be the survival of the fittest."

"They have all been competing with the jet age. Because of airplane travel, people now can go to any part of the world almost as quickly and cheaply as they can get to the mountains. It's almost cheaper to go to Europe, South America, or the Orient than go to Grossinger's or the Concord for a two-week vacation. But they forgot one thing—they forgot to encourage flying. Until they succeed in getting people up in the air by plane or jet, with sufficient landing fields, people can only go by car. Now people are getting used to flying and they love it."

Milton further told me, "I have spent the past five years trying to make arrangements with Mohawk Airlines or some other lines to give us direct flight service up here, but I've been getting opposition because most of the hotels think I'm only trying to help Grossinger's because we're the first with an airport. If they would all help break down this tough resistance, we'd all be flying up to the Catskills and it will be the "Borscht Belt on Wings." But please don't call it Borscht Belt—we've outgrown that long ago."

CONCORD HOTEL

In 1965 I had an hour-long talk with Ray Parker, general manager of the Concord Hotel, the largest and best known of all the hotels in the Catskill Mountain area. Ray is the nephew of Mr. Winarick, founder of the Concord. Grossinger had been the outstanding leader in the resort business in this area, but Winarick's vast resources, finances, and the drive to get to the top and his intensive competition with Jennie Grossinger were well known. It is also general knowledge that Winarick was the owner of Jeris Hair Tonic and a rich man.

He bought the mortgage of the old hotel for $5,000. Recently, accepting an award from the Sullivan County Association, he said,

"I'm still trying to get back my original $5,000 investment." He kept pouring back the profits into the business. He enlarged the little hotel, accommodating only a few guests, to the present giant and leader in the industry, housing more than 2,500 guests. Every known facility and the finest accommodations (two baths in every room), three championship golf courses, an indoor swimming pool, and indoor ice-skating rink for inclement weather are among the facilities. There are also three outdoor pools. An old gag is that Winarick built an indoor mountain; also that one of his pools is for rinsing only.

Winarick died a few years ago. Now Ray Parker, his nephew and manager, is the budding genius of this vast empire. I recently spent 24 hours at the Concord and haven't seen even one-hundredth of the place. Suffice to say it runs like a smooth giant—wonderful food, great rooms, and the finest in entertainment, with facilities too numerous to mention. Everything is here for the vacationist, whether the weather is good or bad.

I walked into a nightclub that seats over a thousand and thought that this is where the show would be. I was told that this was the old nightclub and was shown the new Imperial Room which seats over 3,500 people. A fantastic room—the largest, most modern, and beautiful in the world. I have seen them all in Las Vegas and Florida, and hasten to say there couldn't be anything comparable anywhere in the world.

Put briefly, there are three large, luxurious dining rooms that seat over 3,500 people, a children's dining room, a coffee shop, and late-breakfast room. Those on special diets are catered to. In addition, there is a golf clubhouse, and, of course, outdoor patios.

The Imperial Room, a nightclub encompassing more than 24,000 square feet, is arranged so that every table can view the great stage. There is never a cover or minimum charge at any time. Three orchestras alternate with dance music from 9:30 P.M. until the wee small hours.

Regarding golf, there is the 18-hole international championship course and the Challenger, a sporty 9-holer. And, of course, the Club House. The Club House car delivers players to and from the course.

In charge of water sports is Buster Crabbe, former Olympic swimming champion. One can skate (ice) either outdoors or in—take your pick. Winter sports include skiing and tobogganing, with excellent ski slopes and, of course, a Swiss chalet.

Not to be overlooked are a barber shop, beauty salon, children's shop, dance studio, drug store, florist, gift shop, golf shop, jewelry store, ladies'-wear boutique, massage salon, men's-wear store, newsstand, photography and portrait painting, skate and ski shop, valet and laundry, plus checkroom, credit arrangements, children's facilities, babysitters, pet-walkers, and safety deposit boxes. Religious and medical services are a MUST.

We have dealt mostly with the physical aspects of the Concord. Ray brings out these important points. One particular weekend alone they took care of 400 children of various ages, with 15 counselors to shepherd them. The adults see them only occasionally, for reassurance. The kids engage in special activities including programs, movies, art classes, and athletic events. There is even a rock and roll band for the teenagers.

As for the entertainment policy, Ray feels that the big-name policy will endure for as long as the hotel can afford the cost. The Concord insists on exclusivity from stars, guaranteeing that such headliners as Tony Martin, Barbra Streisand, Tony Bennett, and Connie Francis will not play at any other mountain resort in the area. It is the kind of exclusive contract that Ed Sullivan, the Copa Cabana, and Latin Quarter insisted upon.

He feels that the big stars are becoming more difficult to obtain, such as Red Buttons, Buddy Hackett, etc., because of their demand for higher and higher salaries.

Further, as time goes by, the older names become unknown to the younger generation. Recently Marlene Dietrich appeared at the Concord at a fantastic salary and many of the young people didn't know her.

Nowadays the "hot" names are people like Trini Lopez and Woody Allen. So the entertainment pulse must be on the present-day stars. After all, how many Milton Berles, etc. are there around? Let's face it, it's later than we think and we'd better stick together for there are so few of us left. . . .

In Ray's opinion the other hotels have grown too fast. Most of them, in order to survive, have invested heavily in adding more rooms, renovating lobbies, dining rooms, and nightclubs, plus indoor and outdoor pools and golf courses. They did this to meet terrific competition. (Ray is a bank director, so he is aware of their indebtedness.) Most of them are in debt to such an extent that, God forbid, one bad summer there will be many bankruptcies, with banks taking over.

Ray feels that the convention business is most potent. It brings new guests who are lured to return.

There is a constant need for new ideas to attract guests, new and old, preferably more than once a year. Elaborate concerts with huge orchestras, and such gimmicks as "French Weekend," with French motif, entertainment, and food. A "Roman Holiday" surprised us by attracting more than 300 Italian guests who tasted the wonderful Jewish food and other entertainment features for the first time.

It is important, competing with the jet age and the competition, to offer more to the guests.

Ray Parker emphasizes an important point. Most guys who write about the Borscht Belt emphasize the "good old days," with nostalgic anecdotes told by Borscht Belt alumni. A writer for a national magazine gave the impression that the resorts are like they were long ago, that we cater only to Jews and that borscht is an important menu feature. That's no longer valid and it's unfair to the industry today. He feels that the term Borscht Belt and the Jews should not be mentioned, as this gives the public a different image of what it really is now. As a matter of fact, borscht is seldom on the menu unless you ask for it or it is part of the Friday night menu.

People of every color and creed have discovered that they get more for their money at these resorts than any place in the world. Sure, you can visit Europe, the Islands, and the Pacific for perhaps the same amount of money, but when you consider all the factors— especially where families and chidren are concerned—there are no places that can offer as much at so little cost.

As for the price of entertainment, Ray reminded me when I told him what Eddie Cantor said about the total salaries of five big Ziegfeld stars (Will Rogers, Fanny Brice, W. C. Fields, Bert Williams, and Eddie Cantor). Their salaries, lumped together for the week, amounted to no more than one "Name" gets for one night at the Concord. Salaries have jumped at least 1,000 percent since Ziegfeld's time—and there were no taxes then. So if a performer gets $5,000 for one appearance, he winds up with about as much, by comparison, as the old star who earned $1,000 per week in the days before income taxes, when it didn't cost as much to live.

Obviously the Concord, catering to 2,500 guests or more, can afford the $5,000 fee a star demands, more so than a hotel that caters to only 500 people.

Ray is strongly against hotels giving anything away free. He feels that the hotels should band together for protection regarding giveaways. He feels that it cheapens a hotel and does more harm than good. If golf is included free, you risk hurting your golf course by attracting the hackers and chasing away your good golfers, who refuse to play with beginners and hackers.

The second and third generation now operating the hotels are introducing new concepts into the business. They point their programs toward the young to attract their clientele. The young people's crazy gyrations in doing the twist and other disco dances, lures the interest of the oldsters—who then try to do it themselves.

Weekend guests come up for tumult, which is supplied by a program of continuous entertainment until the wee hours. But the guests who come for a week or more gravitate to athletic sports, plus concerts, lectures, art classes, and audience participation. Dreaming up new ideas is the name of the game, else why would guests pay higher rates to come if more weren't offered?

So you find more tournaments, more big names, more entertainment and activity, larger and better rooms, with more help to serve you.

People like to go where the action is—see other people. One of the most popular "sports" is sitting in the lobby watching people check in and out and milling about. The women especially are interested in seeing what other women are wearing.

All-important to Ray Parker is to ELIMINATE THE WORD "BORSCHT," and buy acts on an exclusive basis. The stars feel that it is the "Palace" and mecca of show business to play the Concord, so they agree.

TAMARACK COUNTRY CLUB

The early history of Tamarack Country Club and the Levinson family is similar to some of the other stories already collected. Dave's father, Max (Pop) Levinson was a farmer in the old country. Because of poor health he bought a farm in Ellenville. He was a tailor and in order to pay off the farm mortgage often used to travel to New York to do tailoring. When he bought the farm, he took in boarders at $5 a week. They had four rooms to rent. He kept adding rooms. Recently, in celebration of the fiftieth anniversary of Tamarack, they invited several of the families who had been their first customers.

Max's son Dave, just out of high school, helped out in the operation of the business. Dave hated the farming business—getting up early to milk cows and feed chickens, so he took over the office. Dave was the only son—he had eight sisters—he took over the operation and authority when the father passed on. Dave has three daughters who helped during their younger days; now that they are all married to successful husbands, they are out of the hotel business and glad of it. One is married to Dick Gerstein, Attorney General of Florida.

The Tamarack has always kept strict orthodox dietary rules and still does, one of the few remaining hotels that does so.

Through the years, the Tamarack has been a leader in entertainment. Many present day stars started there: Robert Merrill, Jan Peerce, Sam Levinson and Red Buttons. Julie Munshin, Norman Toker and Earl Wrightson are all alumni.

Some of the famous athletes and basketball players who worked here are Bob Cousy (Mr. Basketball himself), Max Saslofsky, Alan Stern, Ally Sherman (coach of the Giants football team), Judge Eddie Silver. Rodriguez, welterweight champion, trained there. Rocky Marciano's family lived there while Rocky trained at Grossinger's.

Dave Levinson, aside from being a leading and outstanding hotel owner, has been one of the most prominent figures in the Sullivan County Hotel Association. He was one of the leaders in the drive to take the "borscht" out of the Catskills and put in "culture." In keeping with this thought, from 1955 to 1958 they presented the Empire State Musical Festival in Ellenville with musical greats such as Leopold Stokowski and his famous "N.B.C. Symphony of the Air," with over 50 musicians. They drew crowds from all over the state and country. The festival was sponsored by a few hotels, but mostly by an angel—Frank Forrest, President of Feenamint, who contributed almost $100,000 a year. But the money died out after 1958 and so did the festival. Among the plays presented were "Midsummer Night's Dream" (starring Red Buttons. This was his comeback after his first TV fiasco.) and operas: "Emperor Jones," "Madame Butterfly," and "LaBoheme."

"Murder in the Cathedral" was presented under a tent one summer. Just before the performance, the tent was ripped in half after being struck by lightning.

Famous critics such as Taubman of the *Times*, Harriet Johnson and Coleman of the *Mirror*, all attended this festival and the Borscht Belt was very proud of it.

Dave still thinks the title "Borscht Belt" is derogatory and that the hotels have outgrown it and earned a better name. He is also of the opinion that the old staff and program of entertainment will never come back. This generation is too sophisticated and wise to show business to undertake amateur productions.

It is only recently that hotels opened for Passover. Now the season is being extended from Passover until New Year's. There is a dining room and new nightclub that seats 1,000 people and are doing a near-capacity business.

Chapter 9

Memorable and Embarrassing Moments

*I*n my long and varied career, it is only natural that I would experience some well-known "Bloopers," "Bleeps," and memorable "Goofs." Here are a few of them.

The summer was 1939, the place Grossinger's. I had just been signed as social director by Jennie Grossinger and it was opening night for me. A big night, the house was packed. Eddie Cantor, my friend and cousin, introduced me before a celebrity-packed theatre. I had served as social director and master of ceremonies at Totem Lodge from 1927 to 1938, and had welcomed our Totem Lodge guests thousands of times. You get so used to repeating the welcome that it becomes part of your thinking and speaking, and so it happened. After a very flattering introduction by Eddie Cantor, I stepped onto the Grossinger stage for the first time and my very first words were, "Good evening, ladies and gentlemen, welcome to *Totem Lodge*." All I recall was a scream from Jennie Grossinger in the audience. I never lived down this one embarrassing moment during my entire summer stay at Grossinger's.

This same embarrassing moment repeated itself almost twenty years later. I had served as M.C. and entertainment director at the Eden Roc Hotel, owned by my friend Harry Mufson. The year was 1958 and the next winter Samuel Friedlander hired the entire executive staff from the Eden Roc to open his beautiful new hotel, The Diplomat. I had been introducing the acts at the Eden Roc for one year. The same Freudian slip happened again. It was opening night at the Diplomat. The house was studded with celebrities of every walk of life. Even his bitter competitor, Harry Mufson, and other hotel owners were in the audience. Sure enough, my opening remarks were: "Good evening, ladies and gentlemen, welcome to the *Eden Roc*."

During my engagement at the Diplomat Hotel, many outstanding names were featured. Among them was Jaye P. Morgan, popular singer of the day, who had just recorded my song, "Miss You," on MGM. Opening night, at the end of her act, she introduced me and asked me to accompany her at the piano while she sang my latest song, "Miss You." I graciously accepted, sat down to play, and found to my dismay that her orchestration was written in five flats. I could not read in this key, and immediately raised my hand for a downbeat to start the band, while I called for Mal Malkin, the leader, to rescue me. He quickly sat down at the piano while I conducted, and saved me from another embarrassing moment.

As you can see by the list of my credits, I have been in almost every phase of show business from the time I entered an amateur contest in Worcester, Massachussetts, at the age of 10, until I served as entertainment director in 1960 at the largest and most luxurious resort in the world, the Fontainbleau Hotel in Miami Beach, Florida. Sometimes versatility is an asset, but to some it might be a curse instead of a blessing. Eddie Cantor once said, "I've got so many irons in the fire, I put the fire out." I am inclined to agree with him for my many talents have taken me in many directions in my career and spread me too thin. Let me give you a few anecdotes that should crystalize this thought, or illustrate this point.

I once met a man who after hearing my name, said, "Henry

Tobias? I remember a fellow by that name who was social director at Totem Lodge." I said, "That's me."

"Then who was the Tobias who had his orchestra at the Palais D'Or in the '30s?"

I said, "That's me."

"Oh, but I also remember a Tobias who wrote 'Katinka' and used to play vaudeville."

I said, "That was me."

"Yes?" said this man, slightly confused. "Then who was the guy I met at Grossinger's, and in Florida?"

"That was me."

By now he threw up his hands and walked away in a daze.

Another incident actually happened to me when I owned and operated a summer resort called Cedars Country Club in Lakeville, Connecticut, during 1940–1941. Being a jack of all trades and one who liked to stick his nose into all departments, I drove the station wagon to the train and picked up some guests. I welcomed them, but did not tell them I was the owner. When we arrived at camp, I unloaded their luggage and went behind the desk of the office. As they entered I handed them a pen to register and one man said, "You look just like the driver of the wagon."

I said, "That's me."

The guest looked surprised, merely said, "Oh," and went to his room with his wife.

When dinner time came around, I usually greeted the guests at the entrance of the dining room. This same guest came into the dining room, looked at me and said, "Good evening. Gee, you look just like the fellow who drove me from the station. Was that your brother?"

I said, "No, that's me."

Now he was puzzled, but finished his dinner and after dinner the guests usually went up to the social hall where they enjoyed the show. Naturally when the curtain opened, there I was in tuxedo, welcoming the guests. This fellow looked at me, jumped up and yelled, "Oh no, don't tell me you're an entertainer too."

I yelled back, "That's me, sir."

Feuds Between Staffs and Bosses

The feuds between staff and the bosses were continual, perpetual, and bitter through the years. The bosses would try to punish the staff whenever and wherever they broke any rules or regulations, and the staff would try to get even in some way without getting caught and fired.

Once a staff member at Totem quit and asked another member to ship his trunk full of all his belongings back to New York. He left without permission or notice, and this was an unpardonable sin to the management. In this instance the management decided to get even with this member, not only because he left without notice, but also he had left a few small debts behind, such as waiter's tips, canteen bill, chambermaid, etc. The entire bill didn't amount to more than twenty-five dollars. The management decided to punish him and shipped back his trunk C.O.D. for one hundred dollars' collect charges. In order to get his belongings back, he had to pay the hundred dollars. But he got even later on by shipping a heavy box of rocks and horse manure to the boss marked C.O.D. $100.

IN ONE ERA AND OUT THE OTHER

I know this heading is not original. It was first used by Eddie Cantor when he wrote a regular column for the American Express monthly magazine and then later my friend Sam Levenson took the same title, with or without permission, and used it as the title of his latest book. Sam had been very successful by taking his first publications, changing the titles, and adding to the material, thereby making successful books out of them. Then he did the same thing using the title "In One Era and Out the Other," which fit the contents of his book perfectly as it contained anecdotes about his early days at home and brought it up to date through almost two generations of Levensons. So if Sam could do it, why can't I? I was more friendly and closer to Eddie than Sam was and I am sure he would not have objected.

Memorable and Embarrassing Moments

This section is the story of my experiences from one generation of music to the other.

I had always considered myself a composer of good, old-fashioned, commercial melodies, songs like "Miss You," "If I Had My Life to Live Over," "I Remember Mama," "If I Knew Then," "Moonlight Brings Memories," and "May I Have the Next Dream With You." My brothers Harry and Charlie had also made their reputation with what we call in the music business the "standard" type of pretty melodies.

The year was 1959. I had just completed my first year in Florida as entertainment director at the Eden Roc in Miami Beach. One of the main reasons I took the job in Florida was so that I could meet some of the big singing and recording stars featured there, such as Frank Sinatra, Nat King Cole, Tony Bennett, Lena Horne, Harry Belafonte, and many others. I figured this was an easy way to submit my songs to them, which was the most difficult part of the music business. As a result, in all the four years I was there, I succeeded only in getting Nat King Cole to record my "Miss You" song.

My brothers Harry and Charles and myself were known in the music business as the best song-pluggers. We had "chuzpa" and would approach any artist who could record or feature our songs. But I found in my position as host, M.C. and program director, that I could not bother the artists with song material. Most of them usually came down to get away from the rat race and didn't want to hear any songs from songwriters. They would rather wait until they were ready to record and have their arrangers or managers help select their material. So my hopes in that direction were very disappointing.

When I returned to New York after my winter in Florida I arranged for a meeting with Mitch Miller, head of Columbia Records, and one of the most respected and important artists and repertoire men in the business. He had under his control and selected songs for such artists as Frank Sinatra, Tony Bennett, Johnny Mathis, Barbra Streisand, and many others. I played a few of my best songs for him and he kept shaking his head negatively. Finally, after he allowed me to play a half dozen songs, he turned to me and said, "Henry, you and your brothers have written a lot of great songs since 1929 with great success, but this is 1970 and there is a different audience out there who buy the records. Seventy-five percent of the sales of records today are bought by the youngsters from twelve to twenty-one. Don't you know that Elvis Presley has started a new trend in the music business and Rock and Roll is here to stay? It's the new generation's kind of music and you ought to get with it or they will pass you by in another ten years. Your music will almost be forgotten. Why don't you go out and find a young group, train them, write some songs for them, and bring them to me. I might be interested in a new young group. That's what we are looking for. Most of the artists who sang your songs in the past, if they are still around, are either recording the young contemporary songs or have their own writers and publishing firms, so you haven't a chance. Your only chance is to find your own artist."

I left his office very disappointed and dejected, but gave considerable thought to his advice. I decided to do something about it. I had a good friend and collaborator, David Ormont, who was a high school teacher in Brooklyn. Although he was part of the New York Board of Education, his hobby and first love was lyric writing. He was a friend of Ira and George Gershwin and his lyrics were always high class, well written, but never commercial. Brother Harry was writing with others on the Coast, Charlie was writing with many writers in New York, so I had to find other collaborators, and he was one.

I suddenly thought of Mitch Miller's advice and realized that David Ormont, as teacher and assistant principal at Boys High School in Brooklyn, could help me find a singing group. There were many young singing groups who had made hit records and every high school boy and girl was trying to break through and become a recording artist. I told Dave of Mitch Miller's advice and suggested that he try to find some young groups for me. He put up signs in his school, advertising for singing groups. In those days, groups used to congregate in the lobby or men's room of the school and practice singing. So all he had to do was go into the men's room or in the lobby and recruit some boys. He gave them my office address and soon I was swamped with young groups of singers, mostly bad.

I never could play Rock and Roll, so most of the groups sang without accompaniment. As they had no music or written arrangements, I couldn't help them at the piano.

One day a group came in, four fellows: one black, one Jewish, one Italian, and one young boy about twelve years old, the youngest of the group, who was Polish. His name was Bobby Pedrick. When they started to sing for me, I recognized an unusual quality of voice coming from this youngster. His voice was so outstanding it out-shone the others, who were just ordinary singers. I was most impressed with him and asked him if he would step outside alone.

When we got outside in the corridor I said, "Bobby, you've got an unusual voice and I think I could do something with you with a record company. Could you break away from the group?"

He was surprised and sounded scared when he replied, "Gee Mr. Tobias, if they found out I was auditioning for you without them, they would beat me up."

I replied, "Bobby, just wait a week or so and I'll tell them I can't do anything for them. Then come in here alone and we'll see what we can do."

I dismissed the group with some unimportant reason, and one week later Bobby returned to my office. I sat down and learned one of his songs well enough to go into a studio in the building of my office at 1650 Broadway, and recorded two sides with Bobby. He sounded like a girl. His voice was so unusual I couldn't wait to let somebody hear him and find out if my judgment was any good.

Paul Case was working for the Aberbach brothers, Gene and Julian, as professional manager. Our friendship had begun when I gave him a job as waiter at Totem Lodge way back in the thirties. He was ever grateful, for he told me it made it possible for him to pay his way through college with his earnings as a waiter.

I rushed over to the Aberbach's firm, located in the Brill Building, and played the demo of Bobby for Paul. He was so impressed that he asked me to wait in his office with Bobby and rushed out to his bosses' office, came back with Gene Aberbach, who listened carefully to the demo and said to Paul, "Sign this boy up right away for our Top Records." (They were partners with Elvis Presley's music publishing firm and had just started their own label, called Top Records). I am sure Elvis had a piece of it.

Naturally I was excited and asked Bobby to bring his mother in (his father was dead). I prepared a contract for the boy who was a minor (only 12 years old) and therefore his mother had to sign as his guardian. My attorney and friend Bill Krazilovsky helped me prepare a strong legal contract, as contracts with minors were very risky if not done right.

I signed Bobby for ten years as his manager. He was poor and I had to lend his mother money every now and then to help pay their rent in Brooklyn and for food.

The main reason I got into this flesh peddling business as a manager was so that I could get my own songs recorded and in this way help my ASCAP income. But no, it didn't work out that way. The first thing that the Aberbachs and Paul Case told me was that they had to get the best songwriters for the boy in order to get a hit record. They brought in Elvis Presley's writers, Doc Pomus and Doc Schulman, to write two songs for Bobby's first single. They convinced me that once he had a hit single, they would make an album and then I could use some of my songs. Naturally this sounded logical, so I agreed and they recorded two sides at great expense. I never read their contract carefully and never knew that all the money spent for recordings and promotion of the record would be deducted from Bobby's royalties.

They sent me on the road to help promote the record. It was called "White Bucks and Saddle Shoes," and sold very well, about one hundred and fifty thousand records, which at that time was considered pretty good. I traveled all around the East, *at their expense, I thought,* appearing on such shows as Dick Clark's "Bandstand" in Philadelphia, and with other well-known Dee Jays in Washington, Cleveland, Chicago, and New York City.

Bobby almost ruined his career at the start when he appeared with Dick Clark. Dick asked him how he liked the Philadelphia girls. Bobby, with his uneducated Brooklynese, replied on the air, in front of probably a million viewers, "They stink." We got out of town pretty fast and never could get on his show again.

When I got the first royalty statement, I was excited, for I had heard it had sold over one hundred thousand records, at three cents or four cents royalty for the artist. I was looking forward with excitement and great anticipation to that first big check. To my surprise, they had deducted all the costs of the recording, which were exorbitant, and also all promotion expenses. When I looked at the final statement, we owed them over $2,000.00.

They recorded another two sides, which didn't do as well, and this time I owed them almost five thousand. After two more tries, they gave us up, and I sold Bobby to several other firms, with equal failure.

After five years of time and money spent—including a tour of the summer resorts in which I allowed him to appear with me, and tried to teach him how to sell a song and become a showman, to no avail—I finally gave up the ghost, and released Bobby. He quickly changed his name to Robert John, made a hit record with Columbia called "The Lion Roars at Night," and that was the end of my Rock and Roll career, and the beginning of Robert John's success.

I GO LEGITIMATE

I have mentioned several times before that I have been involved in almost every phase of show business in my life, but the legitimate stage was one phase I never thought would happen. But it did happen. I went legitimate, and here is how it happened.

The year was 1939. I had just read in *Variety* that an old friend and former Borscht Belt alumnus, Max Liebman, had written his first legitimate play, called "Off to Buffalo." The play was all about a group of vaudevillians, headed by the vaudeville headliner Joe Cook and a group of legitimate dramatic actors, headed by Hume Cronyn, who since then, with his wife Jessica Tandy, became one of America's outstanding and distinguished husband and wife teams, appearing in many hit plays and many motion pictures. Both these opposite groups were living together in a Brooklyn boarding house—each with a different way and style of life, and opposite personalities and situations between the vaudevillians and the dramatic actors. This made for a great plot with very comical situations.

The play had just opened and closed after a brief run in Boston, presumably for rewriting and recasting. When I met Max Liebman on Broadway I expressed my regrets that his show closed and wished him luck on the rewrite. At the same time I said, "Max, I've done everything in show business but appear in a legitimate show. This was one of my ambitions in life."

I was surprised when he replied, "Henry, it just happens that I have a part in the play that would fit you perfectly, the part of a Tin Pan Alley songwriter who is part of the vaudeville group."

I said, "Max, you're pulling my leg."

He said, "No I'm not, honestly, you might be the perfect guy for that part. Why don't you come down to our first reading next Monday at the Alvin Theatre."

I thanked him and excitedly replied, "Thanks, Max, I'll be there whether you're kidding or not."

I appeared promptly at the Alvin Theatre the next Monday, was given my small part to read and read it perfectly. My experience in summer stock for years served me well. Max came running down the aisle after the reading (he had been sitting with producers Vinton Freedley and Al Lewis) and hollared from the orchestra, "Henry, the part is yours."

It was a great thrill and unusual experience working with such masters of their trade as Joe Cook and Hume Cronyn. I had admired and enjoyed Joe Cook and his "Comedy Juggling" act for many years in vaudeville, but never had the pleasure of working with a great dramatic actor like Hume Cronyn. When I met Al Lewis, I had remembered meeting him at Eddie Cantor's home once. He had later produced Eddie's "Banjo Eyes." When I told him I was related to Ida Cantor, he became very friendly and treated me with greater respect.

"Off to Buffalo" opened at the Erhlanger Theatre in Philadelphia to unanimous bad reviews. When I met Max the next morning he looked like somebody who had just lost his two parents. To put it mildly, he was depressed and despondent. He had spent many years writing and working on this play, hoping it would do the same for him that "Once in a Lifetime" had done for his friend Moss Hart. To add salt to the critical wounds printed by the newspapers, Vinton Freedley, one of the most respected producers on Broadway, had decided to withdraw from the show as producer. He was the money man and without him Al Lewis, who still had faith in the show, couldn't go on unless he could land another angel.

When Max told me this, I immediately thought about Milton Berle, who wanted to play the lead in this show when he first read the script, but Freedley had chosen Joe Cook. Milton had money and might be interested.

I called Milton immediately and told him the predicament. He said he was interested and would come down at once to Philadelphia and see the show that night. Max was elated and hope shown in his eyes. He thanked me profusely.

That night, after Milton saw the show, he came backstage and in front of Al Lewis and Max Liebman he agreed to buy a large share of the show in return for his investing enough money to bring the show to New York. (I think it was $25,000 for which he obtained 50 percent of the show.)

As a reward for my efforts, Al Lewis and Max Leibman allowed me to write some songs for the show and to play the piano in between acts. This meant additional income and credits to me and I was most appreciative. Incidentally, Milton Berle, who would rather write a song than anything else in this world, wrote one of the songs with me, entitled "You're Fooling Me," which was published by Mills Music Co.

Opening night jitters was a common occurrence to everyone in show business. Every performer who has ever appeared before any audience will never deny it. But of all the experiences of opening night jitters, the worst has got to be a Broadway opening. You know that everyone who is anyone is out there, from the mayor to the lowest theatrical agent and critic, and the thought of just facing such a critical audience is more than I can describe. The worst symptoms are the fear of losing your voice, forgetting your lines, tripping down the stairs, or bumping into furniture.

My entrance was down a staircase of about ten steps leading from the second story of the boarding house into the parlor where I had to sit at an old-fashioned upright piano and read a few lines. I made the entrance perfectly, spoke my first line, and sat down at the piano. Before my next cue, which was to play the piano and sing a few bars, I had a long stage wait and it was then that I first glanced into the audience. The lights of the stage lit up the first few rows in the orchestra. All I can remember is recognizing the man I disliked the most in the music business, Jack Robbins.

I don't recall anything else or anything unusual that happened that night, so I assume that all went well, for after the show everyone came back and offered their congratulations. Then came those anxious hours until the first edition of the papers came out. But first a little usual celebration at Sardi's with everyone congratulating everyone, and hoping for the best.

Then came the bad news, first the bad TV notices during the midnight newscasts, then the early morning edition of the papers. All were bad, some worse than others. Slowly the party at Sardi's broke up as the cast and opening night friends dispersed and went home dejectedly.

I felt more sorry for Max Liebman than I did for myself. After all, this was just another adventure in show business for me. I had tasted many failures in songwriting, vaudeville, as band leader, radio dee jay, and many other flops. But here was a man, a very talented man (this was before his sensational success in TV with the "Show of Shows," starring Sid Caesar, Imogene Coco, Carl Reiner, Howard Morris, and written by Mel Brooks, Dick Cavett, and others), whose main ambition was to emulate the success of his friend and idol, Moss Hart, who with George Kaufman had written "Once in a Lifetime," and had gone from there to great fame and fortune.

He was so discouraged and despondent he even suggested suicide. I kept encouraging him, especially when I heard a rumor that George M. Cohan himself was coming in to see the show as a favor to his old friend Al Lewis. Perhaps if he liked it, he'd invest some money and the show might continue in New York at least for three weeks in order to be qualified to sell it to the movies. George M. Cohan did come to the next matinee. He stood in the back of the orchestra during the entire show.

I was introduced to this great song and dance man after the show by Al Lewis and Milton Berle, but his advice was the final blow. "Al," he said through the side of his mouth in his inimitable style, "save your money and close the show." This he did at the end of the week. And that was the end of my career on the legitimate stage.

RADIO AND TELEVISION

A few years ago my brother Harry invited me to a luncheon given by the Pacific Pioneer Broadcasters. He was presented a Golden Award for his fiftieth year as a member. This club consists only of men and women who worked in radio and TV through the years. Their only purpose is social and nonprofit. It was the only organization whose only purpose was to meet once a month for the express purpose of meeting old friends and bringing back old memories of those good old days in radio and television.

When Brother Harry was given his award I said, "Harry, I'd like to join this club because I qualify in every respect. I was truly a pioneer in radio and TV, and here is proof."

The year was 1923. I was working for Joe Davis, the music publisher, as a stock and errand boy. Brother Charlie had started a music publishing firm with Lou Breau called Breau and Tobias. Radio had just come of age. One of the earliest radio stations was WHN, located in the Loew's State Building at 45th Street and Broadway. The main attraction was Niles T. Granlund, known as N.T.G. He had a talk and variety show and his main attractions were the acts that played downstairs in the building at the Loew's State.

Charlie realized that this new medium had a great potential power in helping to popularize a song. He had written and published a song called "Hot Roasted Peanuts." One day he got a frantic call from N.T.G. to rush over to the station and help him fill in some time while he went downstairs to try to recruit Harry Richman, who was starring at Loew's State. Charlie called me and asked me to join him at the piano. We were known as the "Minute Men," for we were prepared to entertain in a minute. So unbeknownst to us, we became pioneers in radio.

About that time I landed a program at Station WMCA located on the top floor of the McAlpin Hotel at 34th and Broadway. I played the piano and sang some songs and was known as "The Happy Tunester." A scout for the Thomas Edison Record Company heard me and signed me to a recording contract. It was my first and last career move with a recording contract. It lasted only one release. I don't even remember the song I recorded, but I do remember that the record was an inch wide and my contract lasted for six months.

I also was a pioneer in commercial theme song writing. Nat Abramson, who was in charge of the WOR Entertainment Bureau, asked me to write a theme song for a commercial program selling Lake Fish. The singer was Sid Gary and it was a weekly radio show broadcast from the WOR studio annex located on Broadway and 53rd Street. If you don't believe it, here are the lyrics I recall: "Why do the wealthy, the poor and the healthy eat Lake Fish? Fathers adore it, mothers are for it, Eat Lake Fish." I'm ashamed to finish the song. At least I can say I was a pioneer in theme songs.

My next experience on radio was in the "Big Time." The year was 1932. I had the orchestra broadcasting from the Palais D'Or on Broadway and 47th Street. (Later it became the Latin Quarter and the details of how I got that job are printed in the chapter entitled "Latin Quarter.") I had an NBC coast-to-coast wire four times a week. All I got out of it was a trunk full of fan mail and a few weeks in vaudeville after our engagement.

TELEVISION

I also was a pioneer in TV. Here's how that happened.

The year was 1945. It was during one of my periodic trips to California during the winter. At the suggestion of a mutual friend in

Albany, Joe Miller, manager of the Columbia Pictures Albany office, I went to visit Larry Finley.

Larry Finley was a fabulous character who had made and lost several fortunes during his exciting career—first as a jewelry salesman and dealer in upstate New York (Buffalo). Then when he came West he bought up all the open night time on Station KTLA, Los Angeles. TV was still in its infancy, with only daytime shows, such as wrestling with Gorgeous George and cowboy shows.

I walked into his office, located on the Sunset Strip, and waited outside while I heard him arguing with his TV producer. Next thing I heard him shout was, "You're fired." He asked me into his office and when I told him who recommended me and what my experience was in producing and writing back East, he quickly asked me, "Do you think you could produce and write TV shows?"

I hesitantly replied, "I think so."

"You're hired," he replied. "You start at once producing, writing, and acting in five TV shows a week."

I felt this was the break of my life, breaking into the new TV business. I called upon my friends Eddie Cantor, Mischa Auer, and all the songwriters I knew. In four months, from November to February, I wrote, produced and directed and acted in all the shows—variety, musical, talk show, and even helped produce the Western show which was already on. In those days we had no time to rehearse. It was all done with little preparation. I would outline a program and wing it, which means we would ad lib and fake most of the show, with little rehearsal.

When February came around I received the usual letters from D. N. Katz of Totem Lodge asking me if I would return to Totem. By that time I had reached a salary of $5,000 for the summer, plus room and board for my family. The "Borscht" was still in my blood, and Finley was paying me only $200 a week. I asked Larry for more money and a firm contract for six months so that I could turn down Totem Lodge and my security.

Larry told me that during the summer he lost his sponsors but he would like me to stay on for the same salary until the fall, with a promise for increases. He painted glowing pictures of TV's future. Despite the fact I realized that this was a great opportunity to get in on the ground floor, nevertheless I could not resist the "Borscht in my Blood" and the guarantee of a bigger salary and security for another year. So back to the Borscht Belt I went, with the only satisfaction being that I had been a pioneer in TV.

Henry Tobias as he appeared at the Latin Quarter early in his career.

Henry in prize-winning imitation of Eddie Cantor, 1915.

At the piano with the orchestra at the Shady Grove Hotel, 1922; Murray Brodatz (violin), Harry Zimmerman (sax), and Mike Amster (drums).

The Follies orchestra, 42nd Street, New York City, 1925.

With orchestra and Jack Dempsey in New Jersey, 1930 s.

Rehearsing with Arthur Siegel and Eddie Cantor, Totem Lodge.

Working on the Nighttime Blues, 1930s.

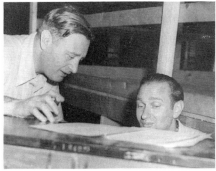

Charlie Tobias and Henry, at the piano, at Grossinger's, 1928.

Cedars Country Club, summer 1940. From left, Nettie Bernstein (Ida's sister), Henry (standing), Eddie Cantor, Jacqueline Suzanne, Irving Mansfield, Eddie's valet "Frenchy," Sophie Tobias, and Charlie Tobias.

Crooning with Eddie at Grossinger's, 1935.

Cedars Country Club, 1940; from left, Irving Mansfield, Jackie Suzanne, Frenchy, Eddie Cantor, Henry Tobias, and Irving Viershleiser.

Henry ~
Was the hole I made a
"4" on or was it a lousy "6"
your pal
Max Baer
1939

Golf with Max Baer
at Grossinger's,
1939.

In front of the campfire at Grossinger's, 1939.

With showgirl, Lou Belson, Louie Armstrong, and Pearl Bailey, backstage at Latin Quarter, 1950s.

Henry with Nat King Cole, Eden Roc, 1959.

At Eden Roc with Lena Horne, 1958.

From left, *the Lassmans with Abbey Lane and Henry, Eden Roc, 1959.*

With Harry Belafonte at Eden Roc, 1959.

And Sarah Vaughn, Eden Roc, in 1959.

Joe E. Lewis, showgirl, and Henry.

From left, *Henry, Benny Goodman, Bob Melvin, Tonny Bennett, Peter Lind Hayes, and the maitre d' of the Fountainbleau Hotel.*

Buddy Hackett, Harvey Stone, and Henry in '59 at the Eden Roc.

With Jackie Leonard.

Johnny Ray and Henry.

Robert Merrill and Henry.

Henry and Tony Bennett with another performer at Diplomat Hotel, 1960.

*From left, Jack Benny, Sophie Tobias, Totie Fields,
and Henry backstage at Latin Quarter, 1967.*

With Lawrence Welk in 1984.

*Irving Berlin and
Jenny Grossinger.*

*Harry Tobias, Rudy Vallee, and Henry in 1985
at the tribute to Gene Autry.*

Henry and
Sophie Tobias,
March 18, 1928.

Celebrating the golden anniversary of Mr. and Mrs. Max Tobias; five sons,
left to right, Milton, Henry, Charlie, Harry, and Nat.

Harry, Gene Autry, and Henry with Vic Mizzy, 1985.

Henry and Sophie
at Eden Roc, 1959.

Harry (left) *and Henry, 1986.*

With Pat Buttram, 1986.

So back to New York I went, another summer at Totem Lodge, another winter writing songs, entertaining at club dates (B'nai B'rith, Bonds for Israel, and others). My song "Miss You" enjoyed its first big revival in 1941. During the war the mood of the public was a sad one and everyone missed someone. So they picked "Miss You" as a favorite and it was recorded by Bing Crosby, Dinah Shore, Kate Smith, and many others, and enjoyed fourteen weeks on the "Hit Parade."

I tried to break through in TV in New York but found it very tough. I did a few small assignments for Bob Smith (Howdy Doody) and Martin Stone (Gulf Road Show) but never did get the big break in TV until 1951.

After I finished a season with Eddie Cantor as accompanist and writer, I kept after Harry Kalchein of the Morris Office to try to get me in TV. I knew that there was a great need for men of my experience in show business. Max Liebman, Ernie Glucksman, and others had broken through, why not me? Finally, with an assist from Abby Greshler on the Coast, and some good friends like Lester Gottlieb and Irving Mansfield at CBS, I broke through the "Iron Curtain" with Mr. Omerle, Hubbel Robinson, and Marlo Lewis. We closed a deal.

I started as producer/director at CBS on November 12, 1952. It was a seven-year deal, but with only 13-week options, with slow raises of $50 each option. It was only $200 a week to start, but this looked like the break I had been waiting for all my life. I dropped all other activities and was determined that this time I'd stick it out and make it. This was what I wanted the most. Perhaps now I could get the "borscht" out of my blood.

I spent night and day learning every angle of TV. My first job was to acquaint myself with all the studios, details, and shows. This I did, night and day: four weeks, six weeks, eight weeks, and still no assignment. I was getting restless and worried. Why did they rush me in in a day and keep me waiting eight weeks for an assignment?

Finally Irving Mansfield came up with an idea for an audience participation show called "The Big Store" that included games. He knew that I had lots of experience in audience participation games and thought I was perfect for this assignment. He told this to Hubbell Robinson and I was finally assigned the show.

After some sweat and tears, we finally made a Kine (test pilot) and the big brass liked it so much they picked up my option on January 25 for another 14 weeks. However, they had trouble selling the show, and weeks passed—no word. In the meantime there were heads flying as the ax went down and cutting was free and easy. They were going into a summer economy drive. I realized that I would be giving up a good summer job unless I got at least a 13-week guarantee. I asked for it, but they refused. So back to Totem Lodge, my old reliable standby, again.

HANG IN THERE, MR. PRESIDENT

During my entire career as social director, writer, and entertainer, I had a strict policy never to discuss or write about politics or religion. I felt that these two subjects were too controversial and personal to be part of my routines. Only once in my life did I stray from this policy, to my regret.

I got into politics accidentally and of all people to be involved with, I had to pick the only man who resigned as president, Richard M. Nixon.

It all started when I asked Richard Mason of Telemark Records (by phone) why he didn't have many polkas in his catalogue. Dick owned a small record company in McLean, Virginia, called Telemark Records. He used instrumental tunes from Britain. Dick replied, "I've been thinking of that and would like to get some polkas in my catalogue. What do you have that you wrote?"

I replied, "Not only have I lots of polkas, but I know the Polka king of America—Frank Yankovic, very well. Frank was with Columbia and Victor for years and might be available to you." Dick asked me to contact Frank and find out how much he would want to record an album of polkas.

I called Frank in Cleveland and he told me that he was under contract to a small record company in Pittsburg, but he was sure he could get permission to cut an album for Telemark. When I asked him how much he wanted, he said $5,000. He said he could make an album that cheaply because his friend Bill Lawrence of Western World Music Studio in Carnegie, Pennsylvania, wouldn't charge scale. I thought he had at least six men in his band, so I figured that this was a bargain in today's market. I conveyed the message to Dick Mason who said it was too much, to try to get it cheaper, and he would try to get a loan from the bank. This was the first time I suspected that Mason was a small operator with little cash. I finally made a deal with Frank Yankovic for $4,000.

My first meeting with Mason was in 1972, before the presidential election. He had called me from Virginia to ask me if I would write a song for Nixon's campaign, as he was chairman of the "Democrats for Nixon" staff. I consented, although I told him at that time that what Nixon needed was a few lawyers, not a theme song.

The next day I was out shopping with my wife and as I sat in my car waiting, I opened the paper and there was a full-page ad by some Pasadena citizens with the big heading, "Hang in there, Mr. President. "I thought that was a great title for a Nixon song and wrote the entire song, words and music, in fifteen minutes.

Primarily a composer, I seldom wrote lyrics, but this song just wrote itself. At that time, November 1972, half the public was still with Nixon, the other half against him. Personally, I felt he was taking a bum rap from TV and the press.

That night I sang the song over the phone to Dick Mason, who flipped and asked me to make a demo. I recorded it the next day at Electro Vox Studios in ten minutes, and mailed it to Mason, never thinking any more about it. The next thing I knew, Mason had sent it to the Republican National Committee, who released the song to the Associated Press.

I heard nothing more until I reached Cleveland on my way to the Yankovic recording session in Carnegie, Pennsylvania. I was awakened early in the morning by Dorothy Worthheim, the distinguished news commentator of the leading Cleveland station. She asked me to appear on TV that day to explain why I wrote a song in Nixon's favor. That morning I appeared with her and, although she was against Nixon, she had me sing it. I found out the Associated Press had put it on the wire and I was getting calls from all over the country, including one from England.

Back to Frank Yankovic and Mason and the polkas. After I closed a deal between them, I started angling and working on other deals in conjunction with this one. My friend Leonard Korobkin was vice-president of ABC Dunhill Records in Hollywood. I first met Leonard during my final years at Totem Lodge back in 1956–1958, when he and his pal Saul Turtletaub applied for positions, and I hired them because I needed them on the staff.

Leonard Korobkin since that time had risen rapidly as a lawyer in the music business and copyrights, first with United Artists, then with ABC, and now was on his own in Beverly Hills. When I moved to Hollywood in 1973 we met frequently. When I told him about my deal with Yankovic he said he had an idea. ABC had 75 polkas in the can including several of Yankovic's. He called an old friend in New York, Larry Crane of Telehouse Dynamics. Larry had had quite some success packaging TV records. Leonard sold him a polka package which contained ten of my polkas. So I got a contract from both Crane and Korobkin for Yankovic to cut some more polkas while he was recording for Mason.

The only way I could get the deal was to offer ABC the polkas at no charge for recording. He also promised that ABC would put out an album of sixteen polkas.

With three deals in my pocket, I flew up to Vegas to meet with Frank Yankovic, who was vacationing for a few days between dates. I convinced him that it would be well worth his while, now that he was assured of four grand from Mason, to make arrangements to record at his and my expense twenty-six more polkas at the same time. It would cost him very little and at the same time he was assured of income from Telemark and TV commercials from Crane, including residuals and at least the same amount for ten original polkas he owned.

We agreed he would finance the cost of twenty-six additional songs recorded, as he was to benefit most out of the deal. It was agreed that I would get the following: 10 percent of all his earnings from his TV commercial, including residuals, for acting as his agent; I would have eight out of twelve songs to be recorded by Telemark and ten original polkas recorded for ABC. The Crane deal would be a good one at ½ cent royalty and the possibility of a big sale on TV. This was an ABC-Dunhill package and they also included an agreement to release sixteen polkas from this package on their Economy label.

I decided to put all the songs I owned into Tobey so that Tobey would finance my trip and other expenses, as it looked like a sure return for our investment. Frank figured that the money he'd get from Mason would not only pay for all the studio costs, but also for his men and the arranger. His profit would come not only from ABC but also from the exposure he would get on TV, which would enhance his box office on the road. I told Chappel Associates' Weiser, Robbins, Fox, and Jacobs on the Coast about the deal, and they were pleased.

Not having met Yankovic for a long time, or Mason before, I was determined to be there personally to make sure all went as planned.

When I met Frank in Vegas in early November, I played over all the songs I had and he was pleased with my material and particularly pleased with my corny piano playing. He liked my Tin Pan Alley oompah rhythm on the piano and asked me to record with him, which I was glad to do gratis. That's how I happened to make the trip east to Cleveland, Columbus, Washington, Pittsburgh, and New York.

Back to the Nixon song.

The story and song were picked up by many papers in the country through Associated Press, and Bob Rausal, public relations director of the Republican National Committee, promoted and printed the song in their magazine, reaching 250,000 people. Mason made about 2,000 copies of my demonstration record, which I thought was awful—only me at the piano—and he began to sell my own record.

Overnight I became a recording artist, singing at the piano, producing a polka album, and singing with Yankovic. I had no idea this would snowball, so I printed a thousand professional single-page copies. Then I saw the possibilities of what might happen. Mason suggested I print a nice, regular copy with Nixon's picture. So I did, including all the songs I had written for Nixon in the past—"Fixing a Date for Nixon," "I'm a Democrat for Nixon," and "Here's to the President" (lyrics by Al Gamse to "Here's to the President, Hail to the Chief.")

When I got to Washington (I had never met Mason in person, so didn't know what he looked like), I had him paged at the airport. Soon I saw a fellow walking with a copy of "Hang in There, Mr. President," and knew it was Mason. I visited his home, stayed over, entertained the local citizens at his home, then flew on to Pittsburgh with him. To insure that the vocals would be good and not only mine, I arranged for Bernie Knee, well-known singer and recording artist, to fly down and sing most of the polkas. I paid him $250 plus expenses and he recorded over a dozen songs with only an hour or two rehearsal. Bernie cut thirty-six songs in one day in Pittsburgh.

I convinced Mason to have Yankovic record "Hang in There, Mr. President" with Bernie Knee. This could turn out to be a sleeper. We did. We called KDKA's midnight dee jay, who invited me over. In a five-foot snowfall I went to the studio and appeared from midnight to five in the morning. The response was sensational. I got calls from all over the country, including Hawaii—some good, some bad.

Chapter 10

The Latin Quarter

I spent so many exciting years at the Latin Quarter in New York City that it became an important part of my life, and so I feel that it deserves a chapter of its own.

I first saw the Latin Quarter in 1925 when I was still in my teens. A friend told me that Archie Slater was looking for a piano player. I did not have enough confidence in my ability as a pianist to fill a position with a big band in the biggest nightclub in America but I took a chance and faked the audition—after all, I was a good "oompah" man and learned to fake with the best of them. With a big band like Archie's, one never heard the pianist much, only his "oompah" rhythm, which I was good at doing.

The Latin Quarter was then called the Palais D'Or, which was the best-known Chinese restaurant, located at the famous triangular crossroads of "The Great White Way," between 47th and 46th Streets, between Broadway and Seventh Avenue, where both streets cross.

153

I suffered through one week's engagement. At the end of the week Archie Slater skipped out the back door with all the men's salaries and was never heard of for years. After filing a complaint with the Musicians Union, they finally traced him to New Jersey where he was working in an obscure nightclub. He was forced, through the Musician's Union, finally to pay back all the salaries after several years.

My next experience at the Palais D'Or was in the year 1932. I had just written my big hit, "Miss You," and a few smaller ones, including "Katinka," "At Last" (from Earl Carroll's "Sketch Book"), "Along Came Love" from Earl Carroll's "Vanities," and already had a reputable name as social director at one of the leading resorts in New York State—Totem Lodge.

One of my best friends and Broadway's leading tailor was Irving Gurian, who owned a men's clothing store with his brother Bill. He had developed a close friendship with the owner of the Palais D'Or, Mr. Hong, who was one of the leaders of the so-called "Chinese Mafia" (Chinese gang leaders). One day Mr. Hong came to Irving Gurian and told him that business was slowing down considerably at the Palais D'Or and he needed an orchestra leader as an attraction. At that time the majority of the customers were the Jewish clientele, so Mr. Hong preferred a nice young Jewish band leader who could attract customers (mostly ladies to the matinees).

Irving Gurian immediately told Mr. Hong, "I've got just the young man you are looking for. He is the leading social director of the biggest summer adult resort, Totem Lodge, that caters mostly to the Jewish clientele. He has just written a big hit, 'Miss You,' which was on the Hit Parade for over ten weeks. He sings, is fairly good looking (although skinny and nervous, with pimples), and is not only well known among the Jewish followers, but also on Tin Pan Alley in the music business, because his two brothers are also songwriters and have written several big song hits by themselves—Harry, 'Sweet and Lovely,' 'It's a Lonesome Old Town,' 'Miss You' (with Henry), 'Sail Along Sil'vry Moon,' 'No Regrets,' 'When Your Hair Has Turned to Silver,' and many others."

He promised Hong that if he hired me, we would put together the best band in New York with top musicians, and even lose money as an investment for the privilege of appearing at the Palais D'Or. I must explain that the Palais D'Or had a coast-to-coast radio hookup and had made several previous band leaders famous, such as Paul Whiteman, B. A. Rolfe, Henry Busse, Larry Funk, and others. The eight times a week coast-to-coast hookup would insure any fairly good band fame and fortune.

Mr. Hong was sold and without an audition he had enough faith in his Jewish friend Irving Gurian to sign me up, for scale. Before I agreed, I was most reluctant, as I did not have the money to invest for myself, and Irving Gurian assured me that we would make up the difference by getting paid from the music publishers who used to pay orchestra leaders who had air time to feature their songs (payola), so they could reach what they called in those days "The Charts" and eventually "The Hit Parade."

It was wintertime and I had no commitment until the following summer, so what could I lose? (Little did I suspect!) I was sure that this was my biggest break and the opportunity of a lifetime, that would lead to fame and fortune.

My next job was to assemble the best musicians in New York who were available. When I went to the union I didn't reveal the fact that I had the contract in my pocket but no band because this was the most sought-after job in the union. I carefully had to hire the best men.

My closest friend was Walter Scharf, who later became one of the outstanding musical directors for the movies and has since won many Oscars for his brilliant composing, arranging, and conducting. He hired the top men in New York, men such as Angie Retina and Babe Solow at trumpet, Nat Levine at drums, Paul Patent, bass, Artie Foster on trombone, Costello on the sax. In order to sign them, I had to pay them above scale and was soon obligated to more than a thousand dollars a week more than scale. Once again Irving Gurian, my manager (with whom I signed regrettably), assured me we would make it all back from the publishers and would be getting big money in one year after all those broadcasts.

I had to reveal that I had the contract to those with whom I signed agreements, and so the secret was soon on the street and everyone in the Musicians Union was shocked to learn that a mere neophyte who had never before played with a big-time orchestra (my only past experience was at resorts and in small-club engagements with pick-up bands) had grabbed the biggest band-leader prize on Broadway.

So we opened with a big splash, lots of publicity and a remote NBC coast-to-coast wire, eight times a week. The publishers, who were all my friends and friends of my brothers Harry and Charlie, hounded me from the first day. I found it impossible to live in the

Bronx with my in-laws and still appear for luncheon matinee sessions at the Palais D'Or, so I moved into the Edison Hotel, one block from the restaurant, and my phones never stopped ringing.

When I got up at eleven in the morning after playing until 2:00 A.M. the previous night, I found all my publisher friends waiting in the lobby for me and begging me to include their songs on the week's program or the next week so that they could make the music list in the Sunday *Inquirer*. This was a sure step to the "Hit Parade." But when it came to ask for fifteen to twenty-five dollars for a chorus arrangement so that I could pay some of my big salaries (especially Scharf, who was my arranger and conductor), they all looked at me in amazement. Murray Baker, professional manager of Robbins, who was Belle Baker's brother, would cry (he was known as the "Crying Plugger"), "Henry, how could you ask my boss Jack Robbins to pay you, when he just made your brother Harry rich by publishing two of his biggest hits in a row, 'Sweet and Lovely' and 'No Regrets'?"

When I approached Joe Morris, who had a reputation as always paying $25 for a plug, he cried, "Henry, how could you ask me for money when your brother Charlie just had three hits with me and more to come, including 'When Your Hair Has Turned to Silver,' 'Somebody Loves You,' and 'Apple Blossom Time'?"

And so it went down the line. I couldn't ask Harry Link or Phil Kornheiser of Feist. They had just published my first song hit "Katrinka" and more songs were coming out. So this was how it was with every publisher. When I approached Georgie Joy or Joe Santley of Santley and Joy, they were shocked, for hadn't they just published my biggest hit, "Miss You"?

All the extra fringe benefits that we had hoped and prayed for, and depended upon, were out of the question. My cousin Charlie Ross was professional manager of Famous/Paramount Music and my best friends worked for Shapiro, Bernstein, and so forth and so on. In the meantime it was costing us more than five hundred dollars a week more than we were getting.

I felt the biggest mistake was that my manager was in the clothing business and not in the music business. If he had made a deal with MCA or the William Morris office or Willard Alexander, or any one of the top managers, such as Louis Armstrong's manager, Joe Glaser, owner of ABC Booking Agency, we would have been able to do our business through them and they in turn would have insisted that the publishers pay us. But Irving was a nice guy who knew nothing of the politics and intrigue of the music business and so, although my mail was heavy and favorable from our broadcasts, I was going further and further into debt.

Then came the time when the summer approached and David N. Katz, my boss at Totem Lodge, was worrying about my returning now that I had become a name in the music business and was appearing on radio and at the Palais D'Or. I finally convinced him through the help of my (*farshtuckener*) manager that it would pay him to invest a few dollars and hire my Palais D'Or band, who would broadcast from Totem Lodge and thereby help publicize and make famous his resort.

When he heard what the men asked for, he went into shock. Finally, when he recovered, Irving convinced him and me that I should share the salaries partially out of my big earnings as social director. By that time I was earning about five thousand dollars for the summer with room and board. We finally came to terms and arranged for WGY in Schnectady, one of the largest radio stations in America, to put a remote wire into Totem, about ten miles away, or we would go into the Albany studio and broadcast once or twice a week. Little did I know that this would result in a near nervous breakdown and financial disaster.

Irving had convinced Hong that he would have first preference to hire the band back in the fall if he let us go, as the summer season was slow. I received permission to take my Palais D'Or band to Totem Lodge. I was to regret this move for many years to come.

First, let me explain that the outstanding professional musicians I had hired at the Palais D'Or were all big names in the music business and had never visited any such place as Totem Lodge. Totem was an adult camp consisting mostly of single girls and men. Most of the orchestra were married, some single, most drank and some smoked marijuana. I never knew about that (and I admit I was very naive for a guy who was supposed to know musicians and show people). I must admit I had never heard of marijuana, but every now and then when I stepped up on the stage ready to start the band I would smell a strange, pungent odor.

Once, just as I was about to start the downbeat, suddenly the trumpet player, Irving Solow, fell off his high-placed chair on the top row of the band. The band roared with laughter, as they knew what was going on, but I didn't know. I thought it was an accident.

You can imagine what these wild, boozing, degenerate musicians did at Totem Lodge where sex was running rampant. They chased every woman up and down the Totem Pole, and many times the owner, Mr. Katz, called in the state police to stop the recurring wild orgies and parties.

In the meantime I had to add to my usual duties as social director, which was in itself quite a nerve-wracking experience: preparing, writing, producing, directing, and acting in shows every night, and arranging the program of activities during the day, at the same time rehearsing the band members for the broadcasts once a week and trying to keep them out of trouble.

Suffice to say that I lost twenty pounds that summer, half my salary, which I had contributed toward the band's pay; and was ready to be taken away in a straitjacket by the end of the summer.

I was happy the summer was over. I was promised the job again at the Palais D'Or, but business had decreased and the popularity of the Chinese restaurant was slowly dying. When Irving Gurian asked Hong for the job again and more money so that we would not lose anything, he was informed that they could not afford more money. I certainly could not afford to contribute any more, so I gave it all up except for a few vaudeville engagements at Loew's Metropolitan in Brooklyn and some vaudeville dates on the road with Jack Dempsey. My reputation from my broadcasts had resulted in these jobs.

I had to come to my brother Charlie to lend me some money, for I was deep in hock. My manager gave up and to this day I could never figure out why he didn't make a deal with a major booking office and really take advantage of the coast-to-coast broadcasts and my popularity. I threw in the sponge, gave up the band, and never put together a big orchestra or worked steady in any place after that. I just confined my musical director activities to an occasional club date or vaudeville date with a pick-up band. The Palais D'Or soon closed due to lack of business, and being the largest of all the Chinese restaurants in New York it was the end of an era of popularity among that kind of restaurant.

When the Palais D'Or closed it was taken over by Connie Zimmerman who tried to duplicate his success with the Cotton Club in Harlem. However, this too was soon a flop and once again the restaurant changed hands, and became the Latin Quarter, owned and operated by two of the most successful and highly publicized showmen in the business, Lou Walters and E. M. Loew.

E. M. LOEW

E. M.Loew was recognized as one of the real giants of show business. In 1940, after opening the Latin Quarter in Miami Beach, which was successful from its inception, he decided to open a new Latin Quarter in New York City. It was an instant success. When questioned as to his "Magic Formula," Mr. Loew attributed it all to a rather simple policy: "Always give the public its money's worth . . . wonderful shows, great stars, exquisite girls, good food, and keep the prices as moderate as possible."

Mr. Loew's activities were diversified. He had a chain of one hundred theatres throughout the East and Florida and was the first to operate an open-air theatre successfully. He was the owner of the Foxboro Trotting Race Track in Foxboro, Massachusetts, co-owner of the now-extinct, famous Wentworth Hall Hotel in Jackson, New Hampshire, and was also financially interested in resorts and restaurants throughout the East. These were just a few of the reasons he was termed a giant in the entertainment world.

Lou Walters

E. M. Loew's managing director and partner was Lou Walters, a soft-spoken man who was born in England. He died in Florida after more than fifty years in show business. Formerly a theatrical agent, he opened his first Latin Quarter in Boston in 1937 with financial backing by E. M. Loew. In 1939, intrigued by the alluring Miami sun, he opened the fabulous Palm Island Latin Quarter. Two years later, also in association with E. M. Loew, he braved New York competition with the opening of the New York Latin Quarter which, since that day until its closing in 1969, became a landmark in Moroccan night life and perhaps the best-known nightclub in the world.

In the interim, lured by the Las Vegas desert paradise, he produced nearly a dozen different shows for the Desert Inn, the Dunes, the Riviera and, after that, the Tropicana, where he brought the famous Folies Bergere from Paris.

Almost every theatrical headliner has appeared in shows produced by Lou Walters. Many a famous star has received his initial start toward success by appearing in his elaborate shows. The stage, screen, and television are filled with Latin Quarter alumni. With a sure sense of showmanship, an eye for beauty and color, an ear for music, and an uncanny sense of timing, Lou Walters had justifiably inherited the title of "Ziegfeld of the Nightclubs."

I first met Lou Walters through my friend and collaborator Dave Oppenheim, who wrote lyrics and special material for several nightclubs, including Nick Blair's Paradise, N.T.G.'s Hollywood Revue, and others. Lou told us what he was looking for, we wrote a few songs which he quickly accepted, and we had no problems coming to quick terms. We were to receive five hundred advance each and fifty dollars a week during the run of the show. When I asked for a signed agreement (I had had some sad experiences with David Katz of Totem, and therefore learned that the only promise worthwhile was a signed written one), he readily suggested I make up my own contract and he would sign it, which he did. I always found him to be soft-spoken and easy to work with.

Back to E. M. Loew. All the time I did business for Lou Walters and wrote songs for a few of his Latin Quarter shows, I never met the man who signed the checks, E. M. Loew. It wasn't until about 1960, when Totem Lodge closed, that my old friend and schoolmate (from Morris High and P.S. 75 in the Bronx), Harry Scheiner, was manager and part owner of a well-known hotel in New Hampshire called Wentworth Hall. When he learned that I was no longer with Totem Lodge after it closed, he talked me into spending the summer at his place as social director and assured me that my work would be much easier, as they had no big staff, no productions, very little daytime activities (mostly golf, tennis, and swimming) and that I would enjoy it. Of course the summer was shorter, only ten weeks, from June 15 until Labor Day, and the salary was also half of what I got at Totem, but the borscht was still in my blood, and I was getting too old to start looking for another job or place.

I knew Harry for many years and was sure that I would enjoy working for him, even though the money was much less than I had ever made. So I took the job in 1961 for one summer and stayed twelve summers—each year getting a raise and finally reaching my old salary.

It wasn't until I worked for him for several summers that I learned that his secret partner was E. M. Loew, owner of the Latin Quarter. He had a home near Jackson, up in the beautiful White Mountains of New Hampshire, a few miles from the famous Mt. Washington. He spent several weeks a year on his vacation, left his family up there, and we became good friends. Somehow he liked me and I liked him. He particularly liked my being a nice Jewish boy from an Orthodox Jewish family and was impressed when I ran his religious services after the summer during the Rosh Hashana High Holidays at Wentworth Hall. He always enjoyed my M.C. work and shows, particularly when I presented a medley of songs I wrote with my brothers.

One day he came to me and said (with his delightful Russian accent; he was really Hungarian), "Henry, I didn't know you were a songwriter. Will you come into the Latin Quarter and see my show? Maybe you can write a few songs for me." I had already told him I wrote for Lou Walters, which impressed him.

During my next visit to New York, I saw his show and made some suggestions for a new finale. He liked it, I wrote it, and when he asked me how much I wanted, he was surprised to hear me reply, "Mr. Loew, all I want is a chance to write your next show. You can have this song for free."

He said, "It's a deal," and that was the beginning of my long association with the Latin Quarter as writer and later as producer of his shows.

Irving Fields, with his trio, was my orchestra leader at Wentworth Hall during the twelve summers I worked there. He was a very talented and brilliant artist and made his three men sound like a big band. He was once elected by the *Music Business Magazine* as one of the ten top pianists in the country. After serving with the U.S. Army he bounded into the limelight by writing such smash hits as "Managua Nicaragua," "Miami Beach Rhumba," "Chantez, Chantez," and many other popular songs. He is a writer and publisher member of ASCAP.

His recordings were bestsellers for many years and he had appeared with his trio at leading supper clubs and hotels in New York City, Miami Beach, and Las Vegas, including the Waldorf Astoria, Astor Hotel, Wentworth Hall, Latin Quarter, and later, for many years, at the Park Sheraton Hotel in New York City. He also made several concert appearances at Carnegie Hall in the 1960s.

As I said, he was a great talent and an outstanding pianist, but also an eccentric character whose personal eccentricities kept him from being one of the top pianists in the country.

When he heard that E.M. promised to let me write his next show, he showered his attention and pushy personality upon the old man, and auditioned for him privately, until E.M. came to me one day and said, "Tobias, would it be all right if you let Irving Fields write some of the songs with you?"

I quickly agreed, for I did consider him a great talent and writer, although I felt that there would be a conflict with both of us writing melodies. I called in two of my previous collaborators, David Ormont and Al Gamse, and together we wrote ten songs for the new show, staged and directed by Richard Barstow, famed director of the Ringling Brothers Circus for over twenty years.

The show opened at the Latin Quarter in 1968 and ran until closing—the only nightclub show that had ten original songs written especially for it, and that ran on Broadway for one year.

Lou Walters and E.M. Loew were having difficulties. Lou was a heavy, habitual gambler who played for heavy stakes at the Friars Club with such experts as Benny Davis, songwriter; Charlie Ross, publisher; and Charlie Rapp, agent. He frequently got into deep debt and once before E. M. Loew had to buy his share in Boston in order to save him. History repeated itself and when E.M. saw Lou getting into debt again, he started to look for a replacement. I always wanted and felt that I could manage and produce the Latin Quarter shows, and so I appealed to Harry Scheiner to make a pitch for me with E. M. Loew.

Much persuasion and pressure came not only from his good friend and hotel manager, Harry Scheiner, but also from his former wife, Sonya Loew, who although divorced from E.M. was still living with him in his home in Boston and helping him run the Latin Quarter. Sonya was a frustrated producer and her wild ideas and bookings, such as the gypsy productions and foreign acts, drove Lou Walters up the wall. They became bitter enemies and Sonya, with her strong influence over E.M., finally convinced him to hire me as he could trust me and I could handle the shows, especially with all the experience I had in writing, producing, and directing, as well as my musical knowledge.

And so with the help of my good friend Harry Scheiner, E.M. hired me at a small salary, but money was never the most important factor in my life. I wanted that job and would have worked for him at any price. The continual salary from Wentworth Hall, which was almost $500 a week, and the $250 per week in the winter, made it easier for me to make ends meet and continue with my first love, songwriting.

Despite my efforts, long hours, and hard work, the business kept dropping off, as it did with all nightclubs in those days. People were refusing to come downtown because of the danger around Times Square, so E.M. started to lose money. Like most successful businessmen, when they lose money, they look to sell out or find a solution.

Lou Walters needed a job badly and had been good luck to E.M. and had made him a lot of money during their partnership years before. He begged and pleaded with E.M. to give him another chance.

E.M. finally condescended, however, he refused to let me go. He told me, "Henry, I'm going to hire Lou Walters to produce the next show. He was always lucky for me and maybe he will be again, but I don't trust him as he always gets into financial trouble with his gambling. So I want you to stay on and keep an eye on him. He will be producer and you will be manager." Of course this did not make Lou happy but he went along with it and took a quick dislike to me, especially when he saw Sonya taking my side and making suggestions over his head to E.M. about bookings.

Finally, Penny Singleton, president of AGVA, through a trick of deceit closed down the Latin Quarter during the Christmas and New Year's holidays, (the only week that they could make some money). She pulled a chorus girl strike, with poor Nelson Eddy as the star picketing in front of the house. E.M. threatened to sue AGVA and Penny Singleton but nothing came of it. A sad ending to a glorious era of nightclubs.

BILLY DANIELS

Here is another exciting happening at the Latin Quarter. The year was 1968, the day was Thanksgiving. I was managing director at the Latin Quarter. Thanksgiving being a usually quiet business night, I decided to take the evening off and see a movie at the Riviera Theatre across the street from the Latin Quarter on Seventh Avenue. The movie was called "Star," and featured Julie Andrews playing the life of Gertrude Lawrence. A very dull picture, but what happened during the picture stands out as one of the most frightening moments in my life.

I was sitting in the balcony when suddenly in the midst of the darkened picture, I heard the sound go off and a voice over the loudspeaker announce: "Paging Henry Tobias. Paging Henry Tobias. Kindly come to the manager's office."

I was so surprised and shocked that I didn't move for a moment or two. Then suddenly all the bad thoughts ran through my mind—"It must be a phone call from California, something must have happened to my wife or someone in my family. It has to be the worst, otherwise why would they stop a motion picture and page me?"

I suddenly jumped up in the dark and leaped down the steep, inclined stairs of the balcony two at a time. How I ever reached the manager's office safely, I'll never know, for I couldn't see where I was stepping and just leaped down the stairs, sometimes three or four steps at a time.

When I got to the manager, out of breath, I screamed, "I'm Henry Tobias. What's up?"

The manager, seeing how excited and frightened I looked, tried to calm me down by softly telling me, "They want you at the Latin Quarter at once."

I was greatly relieved to learn that it was not California calling. I rushed across the street as fast as I could, ran up the back stairs to my office, and saw police and ambulance men standing around Billy Daniels in my office.

"What happened?" I inquired.

One of the plain-clothes men explained, "Some nut sitting in the audience stepped onto the stage during one of Billy's songs and pulled a knife and stabbed him in the stomach. Lucky for him he was wearing a girdle and heavy belt. It saved his life."

I sat down in relief and asked the police to keep it quiet for the sake of the club. To this day nobody ever found out who the man was or why he stabbed him. Could have been a drug addict or a jealous husband, for Billy had a reputation for being a helluva lover with both white and black women.

Chapter 11

My Cousin, Eddie Cantor

*U*ndoubtedly the most important influence in my life was Eddie Cantor, who was married to my first cousin, Ida Tobias Cantor.

I was only a little over ten years of age (1915) when I heard that cousin Ida had married a skinny, popeyed vaudeville actor, Eddie Cantor, and that he was going to visit us at our home in Worcester, Massachusetts, on his way back from Boston where he had been appearing in vaudeville.

The moment he knocked on the front door, which was only used in those days for special events like weddings and special visitors and celebrities, stepped inside the parlor and said hello to Mom and us, I fell in love with this dynamic personality. He told us that Ida had asked him to drop by and pay us a visit. Mom was excited and tried to make him feel at home.

Eddie was always the life of the party and was always "on," as they say in showbiz. He didn't need a stage or lights; any audience of any given number and he started making with the jokes and songs.

Mom had her precious antique dishes hanging on the wall of the parlor. We were always warned never to touch or go near them for fear we would break them. Eddie (we never knew he was a professional juggler) immediately grabbed two of the most precious possessions and started juggling. I'll never forget his one trick. He placed the plate on his straight bent elbow and let go. Just as it was about to smash on the floor to bits, he grabbed it—while Mom screamed in dismay. He invited the family to watch his act at the Poli Theatre in Worcester.

The next night we all went and if you think he had popeyes, you should have seen my eyes pop as Eddie introduced us from the stage. From that moment on I was determined to be in show business in some way or another.

After Eddie left I started learning one of his songs, "I'm Hungry for Beautiful Girls," and the next year I entered the Poli Theatre amateur contest and won $2 for second prize. That did it. I could never be happy out of the spotlight again. I became a ham.

The next time I met Eddie Cantor was in New York almost ten years later, after I wrote my first song hit, "Katinka." He had become a star and I never missed a show or performance of his. I always went backstage to say hello. He was kind, considerate, helpful, and always the first to brag to his friends, "This is my cousin Henry Tobias on Ida's side. He just wrote a big song 'Katinka,' and some day he's gonna be another Irving Berlin."

I worshipped him and always stood in awe in his presence. Perhaps this shyness on my part was noticeable, for later on when I finally worked with Eddie, it took me some time to overcome this feeling. I guess it was his personality that electrified me as it did millions, and in his presence you had to listen, not talk, or you might miss something funny.

I made sure not to bother him with trivial requests or unimportant things. I waited for something "big" before I went to him for assistance or advice.

My first big break was when I wrote my first Broadway show with Billy Rose, "Padlocks of 1927," starring Texas Guinan. It ran at the Shubert Theatre in New York for six months. I was just out of my teens, had written my first pop song, and was probably the youngest songwriter of a show at that time on Broadway. I thought I was ready for the big time and asked Eddie if he would give me a letter of introduction to Max Dreyfus, the music publisher who had discovered Richard Rodgers, Larry Hart, George Gershwin, Sigmund Romberg, and all the best show writers. He gave me a wonderful letter and I went to visit the "Grand Old Man of Tin Pan Alley Publishers."

He was lying on the couch resting, read my letter, and said, "Son, let me hear some of your compositions."

I played a dozen of my best melodies, and then he told me what I already knew. He said, "Son, you have a fine gift of composing pop melodies for popular songs, but you lack the musical knowledge of harmony. In order to become a successful show writer, you must learn theory and harmony and become a thorough musician so that you can compose finer music, ballets, if necessary."

I thanked Mr.Dreyfus and went on my way, knowing very well that I could not afford to study, nor did I have the patience for that. I had taken only a few years of elementary piano playing lessons when my brothers bought the old upright for me in the Bronx after we moved from Worcester, and I became impatient with those simple exercises and decided to learn pop songs on my own. This was one of the many suggestions I regret I did not follow up.

When I opened at the Palais D'Or with my orchestra, Eddie Cantor was there on opening night to wish me well. His many letters of encouragement and our correspondence could fill a book. As I look back at them now, I realize how right he was in his predictions, suggestions, and advice. How I wish I had followed his advice.

My next experience with Eddie was in Chicago. I had been producing broadway shows in my summer resort, Totem Lodge, where I was employed each summer as social director. I had taken these broadway shows and used them without permission.

One winter I was traveling from California to New York on one of my many visits to the family out there, when I decided to stop over in Chicago and witness Eddie Cantor's production of "Whoopee," playing in Chicago at that time. My purpose was to copy the show as best I could and produce it twice, once in July and then a repeat in August at Totem Lodge.

Eddie was most cooperative. He placed me in the wings and played many situation comedy scenes especially to me. During intermission he told me many stories. I copied as much as I could and came back after the matinee for an evening performance. After watching him closely for two hours, I stayed up all night, writing notes and putting together a condensed version which I presented the next summer.

In the meantime, this legalized infringement of the copyright law had become too noticeable after Jenny Grossinger took her entire staff with notebooks to the "George White's Scandals." White notified his attorney, who sent me a writ warning me that any infringement of "Whoopee" (he was representing Ziegfeld, too) would be punishable. I became frightened and immediately called Eddie Cantor, who explained to Ziegfeld that our two performances for no profit in the mountains could never hurt his box office. As a matter of fact he wired me, "I understand you play me better than I, and maybe you should bring your show into New York." Anyway, he saved me a great deal of embarrassment at that time and I was most grateful.

One of my greatest ambitions was to write a song that Eddie would sing and, finally, when he was at the height of his radio career, he had certain gimmicks he used. One was the sound of a duck-like "Quack, Quack, Quack." So Charlie and I wrote a song about it and he featured it. After that, whenever an idea came to us that was suitable for his particular type of humor, we would write a song and Eddie would sing it. Of course, when we wrote popular songs that he could use, he was the first to introduce them, such as Charlie's "We Did It Before," "Don't Sit Under the Apple Tree," "Rose O'Day," etc., etc.

My greatest ambition was someday to be associated with Eddie as a writer, associate producer, pianist, or some other important capacity that could bring me really close to him. But many times the closer a man is to someone, the harder it is for him to recognize one's value.

Here's what I mean. I had already established myself as a songwriter, musician, pianist, gag writer (several years with Jack Kirkwood in California), and producer of some reputation (summer stock). Nevertheless, the only time I could break that barrier with Eddie was when I prevailed on him to let me become the rehearsal pianist for his show, "Banjo Eyes."

When I overheard him say many times, "Gee, I wish I had another good writer," or accompanist, or assistant producer, I wanted to scream out, "How about me?" But I never had the nerve. Finally the opportunity came. Eddie was riding high with his Colgate Comedy NBC TV shows and had just arrived in New York. The papers had printed that he had let his entire production staff go and during one of our several visits I heard him bemoan the fact that there wasn't much talent around.

I still couldn't summon up enough courage to speak for myself, but the next day brother Charlie had a lunch date with Eddie and I implored Charlie to speak up for me and recommend me. Sure enough, Charlie told him, "Eddie, I know you are looking for young good talent to help you in your TV show, and you know someone so close to you who has all that talent you are still looking for, but still you can't recognize it." When Eddie asked who, Charlie told him, "My brother Henry. He can play for you, write for you, and help you produce."

Eddie said, "Well I'll be a son-of-a-gun if you're not right. Have him call me tomorrow morning and he starts with me at once." That's how I finally got to work directly for Eddie.

My two seasons with him were the most exciting and memorable of all my years in show business. Frankly, I was frightened. First, I didn't have enough faith in my ability as a pianist to be able to accompany him. I could not transpose, had to find his key, then go off by myself and study his key alone. He was most patient and although a very tough guy for perfection, he never lost patience with me. When he saw I couldn't transpose, he said, "Don't worry, you have time to learn my key." When he saw that my talents as a pianist were limited, he said, "Your simple rhythm style is just what I want."

My first assignment was to play a benefit for him in an Army camp in New Jersey. He gave me his book of songs and I studied night and day until I knew them backwards and forwards. When the time came for me to play, I was scared stiff and my fingers froze, but Eddie was always smiling at me and giving me the boost I needed. After the show he patted me on the back and said, "See, Henry, that didn't hurt at all. I told you I could do it." From then on it was a breeze.

During our trip back from the camp in a terrible snowstorm, the car Eddie and I drove in turned around several times on an icy hill, but fortunately we didn't overturn. Eddie was the calmest one in the car.

The same thing happened when we flew to Toronto, Canada, to play a one-man show. We hit a terrible blizzard over the Canadian Rockies and even the plane hostess got sick. The pilot flew over Toronto for a few hours in the storm, waiting for a chance to land. Everyone on the plane was scared, including the pilot. But not

Eddie . . . he seemed to be a man who never scared easily, and was always sure of himself and his fate and destiny.

His unlimited energy (he was known as the "Apostle of Pep," and his name suited him perfectly), was astounding. We would arrive before noon by plane, the mayor and a committee would meet us, there would be a parade, with Eddie bouncing up and down Main Street and making with the jokes, etc. After the parade, a long lunch. Then rehearsals all afternoon, then supper and the big show. After the show, Eddie would invite us to his room and keep us up to all hours telling us fantastic stories of showbiz and showbiz greats.

Many times Eddie would wake me on the phone in the middle of the night and say, "Henry, I've got a great idea for a song. Think this over and meet me early tomorrow. We'll work on it."

Eddie was one of the few great stars who always wrote his own material and insisted on doing so. He knew comedy and he knew what audiences loved better than anyone, and although he was always surrounded by the best talent in writing and direction, Eddie was always in every department, and rightfully so.

One day I asked him how many songs he had written. When he told me "dozens," I asked him why he hadn't joined ASCAP. He said he never thought of it. The next day I called my brother Charlie and asked him to submit Eddie Cantor's name as a writer member of ASCAP.

President of ASCAP Otto Harback, at our suggestion, invited Eddie to be guest of honor at the next ASCAP dinner. When Eddie arrived, the thousands of publisher and writer members of ASCAP rose in unison and gave him a deserving standing ovation as a tribute to a man who did so much for the songwriters and publishers of Tin Pan Alley. But when Eddie saw the two pianos with Arthur Siegel and me standing by, and Otto Harback introduced Eddie as a new writer member, he finally realized that he was tricked into coming to the dinner to perform. He took it good-naturedly, remarking that instead of receiving his usual fee of thousands of dollars to perform, he would perform for his first small ASCAP check of $38. It was a most memorable evening.

When the next summer came around, Eddie let me off my TV assignment a month earlier so that I could prepare my summer program at Totem Lodge. He promised that he would come to visit me. During the plans for the Labor Day holiday, I convinced my boss, Mr. Katz, owner of Totem Lodge, that I could get Eddie Cantor to appear there. With entertainment given to our guest free of charge and Eddie's high price, how could we afford it? I showed the boss that he could make Eddie's special salary of $2,500 by inviting nearby customers from Albany and Troy at $5 per, and so cover the costs.

Eddie did me a special favor. He told me, "Anything for you, Henry, but this guy Katz, I don't know him but I've heard about him, and I want to get half of my usual fee, which I will donate to my favorite charity, Surprise Lake Camp." So instead of $5,000, he agreed to $2,500.

When Eddie arrived in Albany, he had asked me to arrange a benefit for the Veterans Hospital which we played without any publicity, and then we went over to Totem Lodge for the big night. Eddie had been warned by his booking office, William Morris Agency, that my boss was notorious for poor payments and bad checks.

When it was show time, Eddie tactfully told my boss, Mr. Katz, that his booking office refused to allow him to go on unless he got his pay ahead of time in cash. Mr. Katz was shocked but knew he meant business and so, as he handed Eddie the $2,500, he said, "Do I get anything off for cash?"

Eddie was a tremendous success and spent a lot of time during introductions in giving me personal credit for his appearance. I shall always remember that night and so will Albany, Troy, and Totem Lodge.

I had hoped to return to California with him as it was always my ambition and hope to land there permanently where the rest of my family resided, so it was a great disappointment to me when he told me that he was obliged to hire Al Jolson's accompanist Harry Akst for the coming season. He hoped I wouldn't mind. Wouldn't mind? I was only brokenhearted but could do nothing about it. I couldn't be angry because he thought that between my songs and my summer job, I didn't need the job as much as the other fellow.

We continued our correspondence and our visits when in the same town. He featured some of my songs and sent me advice and friendly letters. One time he devoted his entire radio half hour to a dedication to the three Tobias brothers, Harry, Charlie, and Henry, and on the air said I was a most talented man, and if some TV officials didn't grab me, they were crazy. I am sure these comments helped me obtain a position later as a producer on CBS TV.

Whenever I went to California I visited with him often and we had long talks. He always told me that a man with my ability should not seek security, but have more faith in himself, that I should have given up the summer resorts long before and gone out to the Coast. I would have made it, he said, like other Broscht Circuit alumni, Danny Kaye, Max Liebman, Moss Hart, Dory Schary, Don Hartman, Saul Turtletaub, and others. Later I sent him a new joke book I was working on.

As I stated at the beginning of this chapter, Eddie Cantor was the most influential person in my career—my friend, my cousin through marriage, my inspiration; and his association was the highlight of my career. I therefore feel that a closing up-to-date portion should be written before I finish this book.

When Eddie died, his family insisted that his services be very private. None of his old show business friends attended the funeral. Not Jack Benny, George Burns, Dinah Shore, Eddie Fisher. The only ones outside the immediate family who attended were my brothers Harry and Charlie, who came out from New York especially for the funeral, and of course his closest friend, Georgie Jessel. Since his passing I, as well as others, have tried to keep his memory alive and have participated in tributes and kept his name before the public wherever and whenever possible on radio, TV, and in public.

Somehow and for some unknown reason his daughters refused to participate in any public tribute or events in which his name and memory were honored. The only one I know who never forgot and kept mentioning his name in his family was his son-in-law, Robert Clary, who always said nice things, and deservedly so about Eddie.

I always mentioned his name wherever I appeared, and spoke and sang tributes about him. My most recent one is the show I produced and served as M.C., "A Loving Tribute to Eddie Cantor," which was presented at the Beverly Hills Friars Club for the Eddie Cantor B'nai B'rith Lodge on September 18, 1986. The man who admired and loved him and respected his great ability was Milton Berle, president of the Friars Club.

I invited Milton Berle to participate in the event and, true to his word, he walked in near the end of the regular program and performed the greatest half hour I ever heard him do. It was a wonderful tribute to a man who brought laughter and happiness to millions of Americans, one of the greatest comedians and humanitarians in my lifetime.

I shall never forget Eddie Cantor and am proud to have had the privilege of working with him and calling him my best friend.

Chapter 12

The Royal Family of Tin Pan Alley

S ome time ago the theatrical bible *Variety* wrote a story about the songwriting Tobias family and called us THE ROYAL FAMILY OF TIN PAN ALLEY. I guess that was because we had more songwriters in our family than anyone else. There were actually eight songwriters in our family: Brothers Harry, Charles, and myself; Charlie's two sons, Fred and Jerry; Harry's son (long deceased), Elliot; and both Charlie's wife, Edna, and Harry's wife, Sophie,—all members of ASCAP.

HARRY TOBIAS

My brothers Harry and Charlie had the most influence in my career. I feel that my life story would be incomplete without at least one chapter about them. I am therefore reproducing the following

173

article written about brother Harry, which appeared in the *Los Angeles Times* and also in the *Music Journal*.

It was entitled "And Then They Wrote . . . Tin Pan Alley's Brother Act."

In 1911 recalls Harry Tobias, "I wrote a little poem and then read an article, 'Write a Song and Make a Fortune.'" He recognized the name in the article as that of a sheet-music publisher. The gimmick, however: the publisher required $25 to provide the song's melody and 200 copies of the sheet music. Never mind that Harry Tobias was 16, and that he was the victim of a come-on. The sheet music to his poem/song called "National Sports" read, "Words by Harry Tobias." It was the beginning of THE ROYAL FAMILY OF TIN PAN ALLEY.

Besides Harry, the songwriting Tobiases include his late brother Charles and another brother Henry and various spouses and offspring who have produced at least one song or two, and are all members of the American Society of Composers and Authors (ASCAP).

Their songs—written alone, with other collaborators or by the brothers together—include "Sweet and Lovely," "Miss You," "It's a Lonesome Old Town," "Sail Along Silv'ry Moon," "No Regrets," "Don't Sit Under the Apple Tree," "The Old Lamplighter," "Rose O'Day," "When Your Hair Has Turned to Silver," "If I Had My Life to Live Over," "If I Knew Then" (What I Know Now), "May I Have the Next Dream with You," and hundreds, yeah, thousands of others.

Harry Tobias is in his nineties and optimistic. "September 11, was my 92nd birthday," says a man still immersed in writing and merchandising his own songs and in listening to those of others.

He and Henry, nonstop talkers both, sat amid a clutter of sheet music, records, awards, trade papers and correspondence in Harry's Sherman Oaks home, and reviewed 76 years in the music business. A framed certificate showed that Harry joined ASCAP in 1922.

Harry began with that first song in 1911—the one that cost him $25. "My only chance to get back my money was to peddle the 200 copies door to door at ten cents apiece," he said. "My brother Charlie was two years younger and he helped me. In those days in the back of dime stores there would be pianists demonstrating music behind the counters. Sheet music was a good business.

Charlie and I started to write music together. He later became president of the American Guild of Authors and Composers and was elected posthumously to the Songwriters Hall of Fame."

When Harry and Charlie began to make money, the first thing they did was to buy a piano for the family home in New York. Henry learned to play it and wrote the melody for one of the Tobiases' biggest hits, "Miss You," a collaboration of the three brothers.

"That was 58 years ago. Rudy Valee introduced it in 1929," said Harry, "and Marie Osmond just sang it on her show." But the three of us only wrote occasionally together. Harry was in California, Charlie in New York and I was in the resort business, traveling all over, the Jewish Gypsy in the family. (Henry was entertainment director at resorts such as Grossinger's and Totem Lodge in New York State, and the Fontainbleau, Eden Roc and Diplomat Hotels in Miami Beach. Henry and his wife moved to Hollywood fifteen years ago.)

Harry's first major hits in 1916 were "Take Me to My Alabam," and "That Girl of Mine," both recorded on Victor. In 1917 he enlisted in the Army and spent World War I shouting song lyrics into megaphones to entertain the troops. He continued writing songs during the '20s and in 1929 he headed for Hollywood.

"The theme song craze in pictures had started," Harry said. "I arrived in Hollywood with Henry in a four-cylinder Chevrolet the night before Thanksgiving 1929. It was just after the Crash and the stockbrokers were jumping out of windows. All the songwriters told me I was crazy to stay, that there were no jobs."

Harry Tobias has had five songs on radio's Hit Parade (the Oscars of the music business, he says). In the early '40s, Charlie had five songs on the show in one year. The Tobiases' songs have been recorded by almost every famous artist in the recording business, including Bing Crosby, Frank Sinatra, Perry Como, Ella Fitzgerald, Nat King Cole and recently, Chet Atkins and Phoebe Snow, who made contemporary versions of his oldies. Henry spoke with fraternal pride. Harry has "Sail Along Silv'ry Moon" on the charts now with Chet Atkins and Phoebe Snow.

Harry, who says he first met Bing Crosby when he was still with the Rhythm Boys in the early '30s, added, "Bing made the first record of "Sail Along" in 1937. This was the song's fourth revival, including one in 1959 by my good friend Billy Vaughn that sold three million records around the world."

Phoebe Snow heard "No Regrets" on an old Billy Holiday record, liked it and decided to include it in an album that has sold one million dollars worth of records. A song can be popular and not sell. Most figures are highly exaggerated.

The brothers estimate that they and Charlie have written at least 1,000 songs each. Henry, whose career has stretched from vaudeville to television [He was one of the first pioneers at KTLA in Los Angeles in 1948], has also collaborated on two books, *The Borscht Belt* (with Joe Adams) and *Twelve Musical Plays for Children,* with David Ormont.

Harry philosophizes that a winning song needs words that are easy to remember and a melody that's hard to forget, and finds many of today's songs admirable. "If you can't whistle, hum or play the song easily, it won't be a hit," said Harry. But some of today's songs, said Henry, could have been a hit 25 years ago. Songs like "Feelings," "The Way We Were."

"We have no objection to new arrangements of our songs," they said, "as long as they sell. You don't recognize your own song, but if it sells, okay." And the Tobias Brothers' favorite song, "Miss You," is ready for another revival.

CHARLIE TOBIAS

No story of my life would be complete without a chapter or paragraph about my brother Charlie, who was the most successful songwriter in the family. He was a great inspiration to me as he was considered one of the best and most successful lyric writers in the music business. He had reached the enviable double A (AA) class in ASCAP. He had five songs on the Hit Parade during the years 1941–1942. Following Sigmund Romberg's presidency, he was elected president of the American Guild of Authors and Composers (AGAC), then known as Songwriters Protective Association, now called Songwriters Guild of America.

Because this book contains many interviews with celebrities and other personalities I met, I think the best way to tell the story of Charlie Tobias's life would be to let him tell it himself.

He died on July 7, 1970, and the Riverside Memorial Chapel in New York was jammed with his many friends in the music business, and every business. I became very close to him the last few years before his death, and wrote more songs with him during those few years than I did during my entire career.

176

It was during his illness that he dictated his life story to me for possible future use. Here are the highlights of his own biographical story and anecdotes:

My early recollections of my introduction to popular music were writing amateur lyrics or parodies to popular songs of the day when I was still in my teens in Worcester, Massachusetts. I would write parodies to current song hits such as "Come Josephine in My Flying Machine" (1910), "Alexander's Ragtime Band" (1920), "I Love My Wife, but Oh You Kid" (1909). They were amateur lyrics, but somewhere in that mish-mash you could see a rhyme of spoon and croon. I guess I inherited the song strain from the days I went on amateur night at the old Poli Theatre in Worcester. (Prizes, five dollars for first place, three dollars for second, and two dollars for third.)

After graduation from grammar school my high school education continued when I joined a musical stock company through New England selling songs between the acts. The piano player in the pit would play the song, and I would make a spiel, then go through the audience selling copies for ten cents apiece.

There's a flashback of writing and printing copies of songs I wrote with brother Harry. We used to go from door to door asking if there was a piano in the house and if they were interested in buying my new sensation at ten cents a copy, or three for a quarter. When I was asked to demonstrate those masterpieces, I'd sing one note of my song on the piano and do a "Sing-a-Long with Mitch." No doubt many a sale was made because of my youth and/or because of my tenor voice, way up there.

I still remember the song title of our first published and written songs: "You Are the World to Me," "While the Moon Shines Bright," and "Cotton Pickin' Time in Alabam."

With that childhood desire of wanting to listen to and learn popular songs, it was but a natural step for me to try for greener fields, and so I latched on as the New England representative for a large New York music publishing firm, Shapiro-Bernstein. Those were the behind-the-counter demonstrating days in the five-and-ten-cent stores, such as Woolworth's, Kresge, and W. T. Grant. My course of duties included covering the acts that came to town and trying to get them to sing a Shapiro-Bernstein song. After singing hundreds of choruses in a music store, covering acts, and singing at a local dance hall at night to popularize my firm's songs, I had the night to myself just to gargle my throat.

While on one of those demonstrating safaris, I went along with my cousin Eddie Cantor and prevailed on him to sing one of my songs in his act. The title of the song was "I'd Love to Be in Ireland, the Day They Set Old Ireland Free." Naturally, I had the opportunity to watch Eddie perform at every show. I learned his routine and then, with his help, I was finally booked for three days at a vaudeville theatre outside of Pittsburgh. I remember I was using all of the material that he used in his act.

Upon my return to New York late that year, I received a tryout at one of the B. F. Keith theatres in Harlem, the Harlem Opera House, and though it was but for a one-day showing; they liked me well enough to keep me over for the remaining three days. That's how my vaudeville career started.

Eddie Cantor later appeared at the same theatre and *Variety* theatrical magazine said in its review, "It was a shame that a big star like Eddie Cantor should be using Charlie Tobias's material."

All this time I was trying to write songs, but as one publisher told me, "As a songwriter, you're a good actor." It wasn't too encouraging. Maybe a streak of stubbornness compelled me to continue writing. The more the publishers turned me down, the more I wrote.

Finally, with a fellow named Lou Breau, I wrote a song called "Hot Roasted Peanuts." No publisher would accept it, so we decided to publish it ourselves. With the advent of radio in the 1920s, Lou and I started covering the radio stations with our latest brainchild. We were known as "The Minute Men" (always ready to go on the air at a minute's notice).

We were indeed pioneers of the crystal set era. In fact we were the first songwriting team to perform on the newly opened radio station, WHN, located on top of Loew's State Building. There were no set routines on programs at that time. Sometimes we were compelled to keep singing songs until they found a replacement, which might not happen for an hour or more. We even went so far as to write a song on the air to titles that the public were asked to phone in.

A man employed by Station WJZ, Major Andrew White, once suggested we buy a few shares of stock in this new baby station (now known as NBC and RCA), for a dollar or two a share, but Lou and I wanted no truck with these new-fangled ideas and, besides, we were broke, so we continued singing for free. Oh yeah! I forgot to mention, we also opened the new WOR radio station located at Bambergers in Newark, New Jersey.

By the way, it was in Newark, New Jersey, while I was demonstrating songs behind the counter at Kresge's, that I met Ray Lew, who played the piano behind the counter. One day a nice looking guy by the name of Danny Lewis came in and I introduced them to each other. As a result they got married and to think, if it weren't for my introduction, there would never have been a Jerry Lewis.

I guess we were the guinea pigs of commercial advertisement over the radio, for they told us that their salesmen bragged about us to their accounts as a good example of what radio exploitation could do, for we sold thousands of copies of "Hot Roasted Peanuts" by continually plugging the song on radio.

At this time I kept writing and trying and hoping for that first real big song hit that would bring me real recognition in Tin Pan Alley. Well, with a song in my heart and a prayer on my lips, I finally played a song to Louis Bernstein, the same publisher who had told me six years back to "stick to your vaudeville act." The song was called "Ho Ho Ha Ha—Me Too." I wrote it with Al Sherman and Harry Woods. I had finally broken the ice with my first song hit. The publishers' doors were slowly opening, not too wide, but wide enough to get my shoe in.

Then came other songs like "Just Another Day Wasted Away," "Get Out and Get Under the Moon," and "On a Dew Dew Dew Day."

In 1929, at the suggestion of Eddie Cantor (who also got wiped out), I invested every cent I made in "Wall Street Stocks." I really was up against a "wall," what with a wife and a couple of kids as my only assets. So back to vaudeville I went in order to pay the rent and food bills.

Then came a thing called talking pictures. Writing teams by the dozens were being shipped off to Hollywood, the land of make believe, but being a lone wolf without a partner, I was left behind. Another writer left behind, bless his memory, was my late and dear friend, Peter De Rose. He was that rare type of tune writer who wrote with his heart. We found a music firm who liked our works (Joe Morris Music Co.) and we hit the jackpot with a song that is still heard today, "When Your Hair Has Turned to Silver," followed by "Somebody Loves You," "Valley of the Moon," etc.

Peter and I were finally sent to Hollywood by Warner Brothers music head, Herman Starr. We did two pictures for Warner, but by that time the Hollywood bubble had burst and musicals were on their way out. So were the majority of teams that left with fat contracts. They were now left with slim pickings and headed east. But during those two years of Utopia for the Coast writers, I had written a few important songs that have since become "standards."

Maybe I was a little luckier than others. Maybe I tried a little harder, and then maybe years brought me what youth can seldom buy, experience. This together with "luck" and good timing, I think, are the most important ingredients of success in most every field of endeavor.

NAT AND MILTON TOBIAS

Although this chapter is primarily about my songwriting brothers, I would feel remiss if I didn't mention my other two brothers, Nat and Milton. Milton, who is ten years younger than I am, and the youngest of the five Tobias brothers, had a successful television store which he ran with his wife, Faye, located on Fairfax Avenue across the street from the famous Cantor's Restaurant in Los Angeles.

Although Milton started his career as a song plugger in Tin Pan Alley, his talent as a mechanical man soon prompted him to leave this uncertain business and go into something more stable. He is now retired and living in Camarillo Leisure World, in California.

My brother Nat was two years older than I and two years younger than Charlie. He was the wise, successful businessman in the family, to whom we all came for advice and help and encouragement. He was the one mainly responsible for my wife and I finally moving to California in 1972. He died in 1973. My brother Milton sent the following "Brother's Tribute to Nat," which was published in the Heritage by our good friend, owner and editor, Herb Brin on November 8, 1974.

Dear Herb:

My heart is very heavy and I don't know how to begin to tell you about my beloved brother Nat. He was born in New York on October 11, 1901, and died last year in Long Beach.

Nat was the patriarch of our family. We always came to him

with anything important on our minds, to receive his valued opinion, support, or comfort.

He was the one who helped keep our families together here on the West Coast, and even back in New York he sparked our Counsins Club. [Ed. Note: The Cousins Club is a remarkable phenomenon in Jewish family life.]

Nat never found it a chore to help anyone; indeed, he pleasured in it. Nat was a Mason and a Shriner, and took an active role in organizing the B'nai B'rith Youth Organization. He was a manager with Prudential Insurance Company most of his life in New York, and came out to California about 1944 with his wife, Gert, son, Billy, and daughter, Laura. Here he joined Acadia Life Insurance Company, where he became one of the top salesmen in the country.

In Long Beach he lived near his daughter and son-in-law, Arnold and Laura Orloff, and their three children, Leslie, Vicky, and Tracy.

Shortly before he died, he attended Tracy's Bat Mitzvah as well as our brother Harry's Golden Anniversary Dinner last December. He was also there at the Friars Club last December to take part in Harry's 79th Birthday Party. He also attended my [Milton's] 60th birthday party.

We will miss Nat terribly. Now the original five Tobias Brothers are only three: Henry, Harry, and myself. We were really an unusually close family, even though there was a big difference in our ages. As our mother of blessed memory would have said, "Nat was a 'Gutt Neshuma.' (A good soul.)"

OUR PARENTS' GOLDEN ANNIVERSARY

My brother Harry once said (I think it was one of his finest lyrics), "Never resent growing old, for very few are given the privilege." Well, we, the Tobias family, have been given the privilege three times in our lives. The first and most memorable one was the

Golden Anniversary celebration that we gave our parents who had been married fifty years in 1944.

Mother and Dad had moved to California at the insistence of and help from all the five brothers. We felt that they deserved a very special celebration, for they had worked very hard during their lives and had finally reached the stage where they saw all their five boys successfully established in their individual careers and businesses.

Charlie and Harry had several hit songs to their credit by that time, and it was a running gag in our family, that one year, in 1942, when brother Charlie had five songs on the Hit Parade and Harry a few, together with one of mine (we three wrote "Miss You"), our mother used to shout to her friends in the neighborhood, whenever it was ours or not, she would instinctively cry, "That's my boy Charlie's song, or Harry's song." And you know something, many times she was right.

We decided that this must be a most memorable occasion, and so the boys hired the Golden Room of the Ambassador Hotel in Los Angeles, and invited not only all our relatives and friends, but many celebrities in the music business and show business, including our cousin Eddie Cantor and his wife, Ida.

What a night! What happiness and love permeated that room, watching Mother and Dad (he was six-feet tall and Mother was a small five-foot-four) dancing a beautiful waltz. As a fitting climax the leading songwriters, including L. Wolfe Gilbert, Sammy Fain, and others, sang special medleys in their honor and as icing on the cake, Eddie Cantor took over the floor and entertained for one-half hour. What a night! What a beautiful memory, what a memorable night!

HARRY'S GOLDEN ANNIVERSARY

The year was 1976 and the place was Hollywood. Harry and his wife, Sophie, had lived here since I came out with Harry in 1929. Harry, who was one who would never let an important event escape publicity, advised me about the coming event and asked me if I couldn't help him celebrate his 50th anniversary by getting some of his friends together for a little party. I promised I would try.

The first one I mentioned it to was the president of the Friars,

George Jessel. He suggested we make a big affair out of this unusual anniversary for obvious reasons. Harry had been a friar for twenty-five years and had belonged to many organizations and was one of the most beloved songwriters in Hollywood. I then realized that this was an occasion that shouldn't be treated lightly.

After contacting several heads of several of the organizations Harry belonged to, such as the Eddie Cantor B'nai B'rith Lodge, the Hollywood Comedy Club, ASCAP, AGAC, Pacific Pioneers Broadcasters, the National Academy of Motion Pictures, Writers Hall of Fame, the American Legion, and others, I found they were all most enthusiastic about making a big night of this event, one that Harry and his wife deserved and one that would be remembered for a long time.

I felt that the only place to hold such a celebration was at Harry's synagogue, Adat Ari El, of which he had been a distinguished member for twenty-five years. I met with the Board of Directors and told them of my plans. They readily consented to give me a night and give me artistic freedom to produce a show, for which they would charge five dollars a ticket for the benefit of their synagogue. (Every synagogue needs money.)

I had been in Hollywood four years and found it a tough town to break through, especially in show business. Although many of my friends and proteges had made it in a big way, I was still struggling and trying to make a reputation in this town. Sure I was a big man in the summer resort business back East and had written a few songs, but this was Hollywood, the big time, and this was the first opportunity I had to prove my talents as a producer. Besides, I loved Harry, and wanted to produce an evening that would be remembered in this town.

I started to round up publicity men, production assistants, and the best music and talent available. Guests are still talking about it years later.

It was one of my greatest achievements since moving to Hollywood, or I might add, in my entire career, for all my friends and former Borscht Belt Alumni who have made good in this town helped me to put it over. I mean friends of many years, such as Mickey Katz, featuring Mannie Klein at the trumpet (Mannie graduated from Morris High School with me). Assisting me in the production were Saul Turtletaub, Leonard Korobkin, Ernie Glucksman, Johnnie Francis; songwriters Sammie Fain, John Green, Evans and Livingston, Bernie Wayne, Eddy Manson, Joe

Myrow, Ben Oakland, and John Paul Webster. And performers Nick Lucas, Benney Lessey, Pinky Tomlin, Roberta Sherwood, and Cantor Michaelson, of the Adat Ari El Temple. I had finally shown Hollywood I could produce as well as write, and felt that I had broken the impossible charmed circle of Hollywood.

MY OWN GOLDEN ANNIVERSARY

As this chapter was being written, we were approaching the end of a very sad year, 1978. One of the greatest tragedies of our lives had happened in July 1978, when my only daughter, Phylis, lost her husband Erwin M. Brown, who died on July 21 after a long illness. He had been ill for some time since falling off a tall ladder in his father's furniture store some six years before. He had gone to many doctors and many hospitals, and some diagnosed his illness as multiple sclerosis (M.S.), nerve damage on his spine caused by the fall, high blood pressure, and many other illnesses. The diagnosis was never fully determined or proved.

During all this time my wife had spent much time with our daughter in Pasadena to help her during her husband's illness. He had built one of the largest furniture stores in Pasadena, Ethan Allen's Jamestown Manor, and my daughter and their sons Tim, Mitchell, and Kelly, helped him.

Getting back to our wedding anniversary. I realized during all this that on March 18, 1978, my wife and I would be celebrating our fiftieth wedding anniversary, but how could I plan such a happy event with such sadness and unhappiness going on in my daughter's home? Despite the circumstances, I was determined not to let this happy occasion pass by without some celebration. For as brother Harry said, "Very few are blessed with fifty years of marriage."

I decided to prepare a modest party without the knowledge or consent of my wife. So quietly and secretly I reserved my synagogue's small ballroom at Hollywood Beth El Temple in Hollywood, right next door to where we lived. While my wife stayed in Pasadena with our daughter, I prepared all the details, including a beautiful invitation. When it was ready, the secret had to be broken. I mailed an invitation special delivery to my wife and told her very sternly that despite the circumstances, I had to bring some happiness to her and the family on this special occasion. She reluctantly consented (for I had paid a deposit and everything was set). Despite his illness, my son-in-law came with our daughter and their three boys to the temple early Saturday morning, March 18, and participated in the religious ceremony conducted by Rabbis Wagner and Levin of the Beth El Temple.

After the shabbat synagogue services our family and guests, including some of my songwriting friends, Sammy Fain, Dan Shapiro, Bernie Wayne, Jerry Livingston, Sammy Lerner, old friends like Benney Lessey, Nick Lucas, Roberta Sherwood, Jerry Rosen, Ernie Glucksman, Saul Turtletaub, Leonard Korobkin, Cantor Katzman (the cantor of the synagogue who had performed at our family happy events, bar mitzvahs, and weddings), enjoyed an elaborate luncheon.

After the luncheon Dan Shapiro took over as M.C. and read some telegrams from close friends who couldn't make it, Milton Berle, ASCAP president Stanley Adams, and many others.

SUMMING IT ALL UP

"If I Had My Life To Live Over," "I'd do the same things again". . . . Those are the title and opening lines of the chorus of one of my most popular songs. I guess they sum up my life as well as anything I can think of.

"No Regrets" was the title of one of my brother Harry's biggest hits. If anyone says there are "no regrets" in their life, he is not telling the truth. Now that I have summed up the highlights of my life in this book, I will try to tell you some of "my regrets."

I regret first that my career in the East took me away from spending more time with my family. My only daughter, Phylis, married a very successful businessman in Pasadena and had three wonderful sons, Tim, Mitchell, and Kelly. Although my wife and I spent as much time as possible visiting them in California, nevertheless I regret not spending more time watching and enjoying my three grandchildren grow up. I do regret that I missed the best years of my life. I wish I had spent more time there.

I also regret not having spent more time writing songs. I loved writing songs and had the good fortune of writing with some of the greatest writers in those early days. I even wrote a Broadway show while just out of my teens, but the "Broscht Was in My Blood" and I loved producing, directing, and performing. As my friend Max Liebman once said, "Where else can you function for at least ten weeks a year without the aggravating obstacles that plague a professional in our business? Where else can you reach an audience without interference, without compromise, without those stifling regulations and phony traditions and without the wise guys' slant on the box office or your image?"

Perhaps if I had spent more time writing songs I might have had more hits to my credit and my ASCAP ratings would have made me more financially secure as I grew older. But I found writing songs so easy that I made it a part-time job. It was my cousin Eddie Cantor who once told me, "You have so many irons in the fire, you keep putting the fire out." He was right. But, "No Regrets."

When I balance the scales and look at "My Blessings," I realize that if I had spent less time producing and directing and performing, I might never have had the pleasure and thrill of working with and meeting such greats as Eddie Cantor, Milton Berle, Frank Sinatra, Jerry Lewis, Harry Belafonte, Lena Horne, Nat King Cole, Elvis Presley. Nor would I have had the thrill of bragging that I was the only pianist who accompanied Eddie Cantor, Al Jolson, Georgie Jessel, and Mae West. And how many can boast of having breakfast at the White House with Franklin D. Roosevelt, or appearing at Carnegie Hall, or doing a one-man concert at the Smithsonian Institution, and appearing in person on almost every important TV and radio station in the country? Or boast of having a song on the Hit Parade for twenty weeks? ("Miss You")

Not too many people have the good fortune of being able to do what they love to do best, during their entire life. I consider myself one of those who had.

In closing, I can only repeat what I wrote in my "Acknowledgments" and again thank all the people without whom this book would not be possible.

In summing it all up, I repeat: "If I had my life to live over, I'd still do the same things again. . . ."

HENRY TOBIAS CREDITS
Best Known Popular Songs

Miss You . . .If I Had My Life to Live Over . . . If I Knew Then . . . I Remember Mama . . . Katinka . . . Moonlight Brings Memories . . . May I Have the Next Dream with You . . . Moon on My Pillow . . . Easter Sunday With You . . . A Man Needs to Know . . . At Last . . . The Bowling Song . . . The Ski Song . . . Brother . . . Rolleo Rolling Along . . . Along Came Love . . . Cookin' Breakfast for the One I Love . . . Go to Sleepy Little Baby . . . Hello Sunshine Hello . . . Hang in There Mr. President . . . Sweet Pete Rose . . . Never Resent Growing Old, and many more. . . .

Theme Songs

Milton Berle . . . "Here Comes the Berle"
Jackie Gleason . . . "And Away We Go"
Eddie Cantor . . . "The Quack Song"
Judy Canova . . . "Go to Sleepy Little Baby"
Sammy Kaye . . . "Our Sunday Serenade"
Brotherhood Week . . . "Brother" (N.C.C.& J.)
Movie Industry . . . "Let's Go to the Movies"

187

State of Wyoming . . . "Wonderful Wyoming"

Ski Association . . . "Let's Go Skiing"

War Effort . . . "Buy More Defense Stamps" . . . "We've Just Begun to Fight" . . . "Write a Letter to Boys"

Jimmy Durante . . . "Me and My Song"

President Nixon . . . "Hang in There Mr. President"

Hotel Theme Songs . . . Grossingers . . . Fontainebleau . . . Diplomat . . . Eden Roc . . . Totem Lodge . . . Cedars . . . Wentworth Hall

Broadway Shows

Billy Rose's Padlocks . . . (Songs) "If I Had a Lover" "Let's Make Whoopee" . . . "Brass Button Blues" . . . "It's Tough to Be a Hostess in a Broadway Cabaret."

Vanities (1932) . . . "Along Came Love"

Sketch Book (1938) . . . "At Last"

Off to Buffalo (1938) . . . "I'm Sorry Dear" . . . "Ain't That Something"

Movies

The Rose (Bette Middler) . . . "I've Written a Letter to Daddy"

What Ever Happened to Baby Jane (Bette Davis) . . . "What Ever Happened to Daddy?"

Timber Timber Timber . . . "She Has What it Takes" . . .

Little Miss Nobody . . . "Then Came the Indians"

Be Yourself . . . "Cookin' Breakfast for the One I Love"

Night Club Revues

Latin Quarter Revue Tonight's the Night (1966–67) "Tonight's the Night" . . . "Champagne" . . . "A Little Bird Told Me So" . . . "Jungle Fantasy" . . . "Hoot Mon"

Latin Quarter Revue (1945) . . . "Sugar and Spice" . . . "I Lost My Man" . . . Paris Is Paris Again" . . . "Sophie Tucker for President"

New York World's Fair N.T.G.'s Congress of Beauty Revue . . . "Is It Just an Illusion" . . . "You're the Fairest of the Fair" . . . "Hello Sucker" . . . "Get Hot with Red White and Blue" . . . "Give the Girl a Big Hand"

Paradise Revue (1938) "Swingin' with the Rain" . . . "You Walked Out of the Picture" . . . "Things They Do in Hollywood"

Hollywood Revels (1937) "There's Something 'Bout the Wind" . . . "Say It with Your Eyes" . . . "When We Met in Paris" . . . "The Pigmy Dance"

L.A Senior Citizen Show *Go Like Sixty* (1980–1984) songs in collaboration with Laura Manning) "Go Like Sixty" . . . "Old People" . . . "You're As Young As You Feel" . . . "Grandma" . . . "Grandma's Aren't What They Used to Be" . . . "You're Never Too Old to Be Kissed" (with Harry Tobias) . . . "The Old Square Dance Is Back Again" (with Don Reid) . . . "Act Your Age" (with Stanley Ralph Ross) . . . "A Man Needs to Know" (with Suellen Fried) . . . "Stop Worrying" (with Harry Tobias) . . . "Never Resent Growing Old" (with Harry Tobias) . . . "Prepare for Retirement" (with Maxine Manners) . . . "Oh! Yeah! You Did It" . . . "Treasures"

Recordings of Henry Tobias Songs by Artist and Label

TITLE	ARTIST	LABEL	COLLABORATOR
Miss You	Bing Crosby	DECCA	Harry &
	Rudy Vallee	RCA	Charles
	Sammy Kaye	RCA	Tobias
	Eddy Howard	Columbia	
	McGuire	Coral	
	Sisters	Columbia	
	Ray Conniff	Capitol	
	Nat King Cole	Decca	
	Mills Brothers	MGM	
	Art Mooney	Columbia	
	Ray Conniff	RCA	
	Singers	RCA	
	Les Elgart	RCA	
	Freddy Martin	RCA	
	Wayne King	RCA	
If I Had My Life to Live Over	Eddy Arnold	RCA	Moe Jaffe &
	Lou Rawls	Capitol	Larry Vincent
	Buddy Clark	Columbia	
	Kate Smith	MGM	

	Gordon MacRae	Apollo Repriese	
	Guy Mitchell	Repriese	
	Bob Eberle & Song Spinners	Pye Records	
	Max Bygraves	London	
The Sleep Song	Glenn Miller	RCA	Don Reid
I Remember Mama	Andrew Sisters Lennon Sisters	DECCA DOT	Charlie Tobias
Cookin' Breakfast for the One I Love	Fanny Brice	RCA	Billy Rose
Moon on My Pillow	Jimmy Dorsey Billy Vaughn	DECCA DOT	Elliot & Charles Tobias
Hello Sunshine Hello	Eddie Cantor	RCA	Charles Tobias & Jack Murray
Wedding of the Birds	Paul Whiteman	RCA	Harry Tobias & Charles Kisco
If I Knew Then	Ray Conniff	Columbia	Harry Tobias & Charles Kisco
Moonlight Brings Memories	Ray Conniff Billy Vaughn	Columbia DOT	Harry & Charles Tobias
May I Have the Next Dream with You	Jerry Vale Al Martino Malcolm Roberts	Columbia Curb Roulette	Harry & Charles Tobias
Katinka	Vaughn Monroe George Olsen	RCA RCA	Benee Russell
I Used to Be Her One and Only	Sammy Kaye	RCA	Harry & Charles Tobias

INDEX